THE BOOK OF CLARITY

THE BOOK OF CLARITY

BUILDING YOUR DREAM STARTUP USING FIRST PRINCIPLES THINKING

PARAS CHOPRA

ILLUSTRATIONS BY AAKANKSHA GAUR

HARPER BUSINESS

First published in India by Harper Business 2025
An imprint of HarperCollins *Publishers*
HarperCollins *Publishers* India, Cyber City,
Building 10-A, Gurugram, Haryana – 122002, India
www.harpercollins.co.in

2 4 6 8 10 9 7 5 3 1

P-ISBN: 978-93-6989-882-4
E-ISBN: 978-93-6569-679-0

Typeset in 11.5/15.2 Adobe Garamond Pro
by HarperCollins *Publishers* India Pvt. Ltd

Printed and bound at
Replika Press Pvt. Ltd.

FSC
www.fsc.org
MIX
Paper | Supporting responsible forestry
FSC™ C016779

This book is produced from independently certified FSC® paper to ensure responsible forest management.

HarperCollins *Publishers*, Macken House, 39/40 Mayor Street Upper, Dublin 1, D01 C9W8, Ireland

To the love of my life and the illustrator of this book, Aakanksha, to my cat Orbit and to you, my dear entrepreneur, without whom the world economy will come to a standstill

CONTENTS

INTRODUCTION

Most startups die. Some die because they never find their product-market fit. Some collapse due to co-founder issues. And some because they fail to raise funds.

However, these are not among the top reasons for startup failure. That honour goes to your brain. How many ideas have you killed in your mind because you could never gain the confidence that they would work out?

Most startups die at the idea stage itself. And those that don't die this way, die soon after, in one of the many, many different ways startups are known to fail. But it doesn't have to be this way. There's no ironclad law of the universe driving the high failure rate of new companies.

The collection of frameworks (or mental models, if you are a nerd like me) that make up this book come from deep introspection of my own entrepreneurship career, which started when I was fifteen.

My father had taken out a loan to get home a spanky new 388 MHz Cyrix computer with a mind-blowing 4.3 GB hard disk. After wasting a few evenings on games, I asked my dad what else I could do with this new toy, and he introduced me to the glorious world of Visual Basic 6.0.

Games be damned, pretty soon, I was hooked on creating software programs of my own in Visual Basic. I'd drag some buttons, put some labels, write some code, and as I would press 'Run', my imagination would come alive, as something concrete in the world.

The excitement of creation is why startups are so alluring. Something doesn't exist yet and then, thanks to you, it becomes a very real thing. Then, if you're successful, people start taking what you created for granted, as if it is how the world always has been. It's amazing that literally everything we interact with—Google, Uber, Instagram—was once merely an idea inside someone's head.

As a creator, one has an uncontrollable urge to show their creations to someone, which is what drove me to upload the software I was building on the web. I wanted a name for my website, and my dad suggested the name 'NaramCheez' (which apparently is 'soft-ware' in Hindi). Physically, I was in Rohini, a sleepy suburb in north-west Delhi known for bankers and teachers. But, mentally, as a fifteen-year-old computer nerd, I felt closer to teenage hackers in the Bay Area. (My friends in the neighbourhood gradually stopped inviting me to play cricket. I should have known better—not everyone finds the origin stories of Apple, HP, Yahoo and Google a fascinating topic.)

NaramCheez failed, but the fun and enthusiasm that came along with creation didn't. I attempted multiple startups during my college days. All these—Precimark, MyJugaad.in, Kroomsa—failed too.

With each failure, my frustration rose. I was constantly asking myself: why did all the internet startups I was reading about on *TechCrunch* not fail but mine always did?

This book is an attempt to give a convincing answer to my past self as it was attempting one startup idea after another. At that time, my startup failures seemed completely random and baffling. I was studying engineering back then, and my books contained formulas for building bridges that won't fall apart when built with almost 100 per cent confidence.

Why couldn't a similar book exist for startups? One that appeals to intelligence more than the heart. One that breaks down entrepreneurship from first principles. One that gives the student a definitive edge in his/her startup attempt. One that prevents the death of startups at the idea stage and later, during its first few years.

I wrote this book as a gift to myself, if ever we invent a time machine and I find myself as a first-time entrepreneur. I wanted a book that appealed to the first-principles hungry engineer within me, so I wrote one.

This book won't guarantee the success of your startup. The zero-to-one journey is an act of creativity that can't be fully codified like a bridge getting built. If we could, big companies would hire consultants to launch new products instead of acquiring startups. But big companies often suck at launching new products, which implies startup success is *hard*.

But that doesn't mean that your startup journey has to be in total blindness. Each framework in this book will give you a new way of looking ahead. My goal is to give you lots of aha moments as you read the book. By the end of the book, you will have a toolkit of perspectives to think about and plan your startup towards success.

If all I had in my career was startup failures, I would have written only about what not to do. But many frameworks you'll encounter in the book also recommend what to do. The source of such insights is the contrast between my many failures and Wingify, my fifth attempt at starting up that ended up working out for me.

After getting my engineering degree, I got a job and told my boss on the first day itself that I'll be working on my startup on the side and will quit if it works out. But I didn't expect much.

Previous failures had battered my ambitions and now, instead of hoping my next startup would become a Google, all I wanted from it was Rs 50,000 per month (approx $1,000 at that time). This amount of money was equal to my salary, and if Wingify (my new startup) would give me that, I'd quit my job and finally break the jinx of failures.

A year of grind later, when I launched pricing for Wingify's initial product, Visual Website Optimizer, I made $4,000 in the first month.

Four times the success threshold I had set for myself!

Woohoo! Even if my revenue never grew beyond this, I would have been happy. But the next month, it doubled. Then it doubled again. It kept doubling, and within eighteen months, it hit a million dollars.

Fast-forward to today, Wingify is doing an annual run rate upwards of Rs 400 crore (approx. $50 million). I'm grateful to everyone who helped build it with me. The fifteen-year–long journey of Wingify has given me enough fodder to think about what went right with it.

The lessons I derive in this book are grounded in business fundamentals and are free of distortions caused by VC funding, because I never raised external funding for Wingify. The entire growth of my startup so far is bootstrapped. My investment in Wingify was a Rs 200 domain name and Rs 500 for server hosting.

In fact, the total investment for the Rs 400 crore revenue company was very similar to the Rs 0 revenue-earning startups that failed. What made the difference then? This book attempts to answer that. To be clear, the book isn't about my startup journey. Sure, I use some personal anecdotes in the chapters that follow. But my main attempt is to derive universally applicable frameworks that you—the reader—can apply in your startup journey to increase the odds away from failure and towards massive success.

As my aim is to tell you about frameworks behind successful startups, I will also dissect many other successful startups and see what made them successful.

I understand the risk of using examples from currently successful companies. Tomorrow, they may not even exist. Even Wingify could have its Kodak Moment. Well, given long enough, all companies die. But the prospect of future failure shouldn't diminish the golden lessons that successful companies have to teach us today.

So, get ready to look at the world of business and startups in a new way. Get ready for a perspective that lifts the fog on your windscreen and helps you clearly see whether your startup is headed for the cliff or for the chequered flag.

THIS BOOK REQUIRES THINKING

The best way to consume non-fiction books, like this one, is to read them holding a pen or a pencil. I hope you agree that the point of such books isn't reading, but comprehension. There are no brownie points for finishing a book and not remembering anything from it.

But, unfortunately, that's how many of us read. We rush through books as if finishing them is more important than taking valuable lessons. I hope you read this book differently. To get the most out of this book, I recommend you the following:

a) Scribble on the book heavily. Underline or highlight ideas that appeal to you. A soiled book is a well-read book.
b) Read it at a slow pace. Think and reflect as you go along. Ask yourself how would you apply the frameworks? What do the different ideas remind you of? Can you think of more examples?

As an avid reader of non-fiction books myself, to truly understand a book, I must try to teach key ideas in it to others. So, for the last many years, I've made a rule for myself: If I don't make notes on a book, I consider not having read it.

I recommend the same to you. The best way to remember what you like in the book is to teach it to others. You can do this by publishing your notes online or on social media.

Another tip I have on reading is to re-read the books you like multiple times. Each time you read a book, it compiles in your head differently. As your life and career circumstances change, you absorb the same ideas differently. So, if this book appeals to you this time, keep it aside and come back to it in a year or so. I'm sure you will have fresh takeaways from it.

> **Remember:** the point of reading non-fiction is to understand. And you don't understand what you can't explain.

PART 1

KNOW YOUR PLAYGROUND

CAPITALISM REWARDS RARE AND VALUABLE

You create value when you fulfil people's desires substantially better than the existing options out there (from competitors).

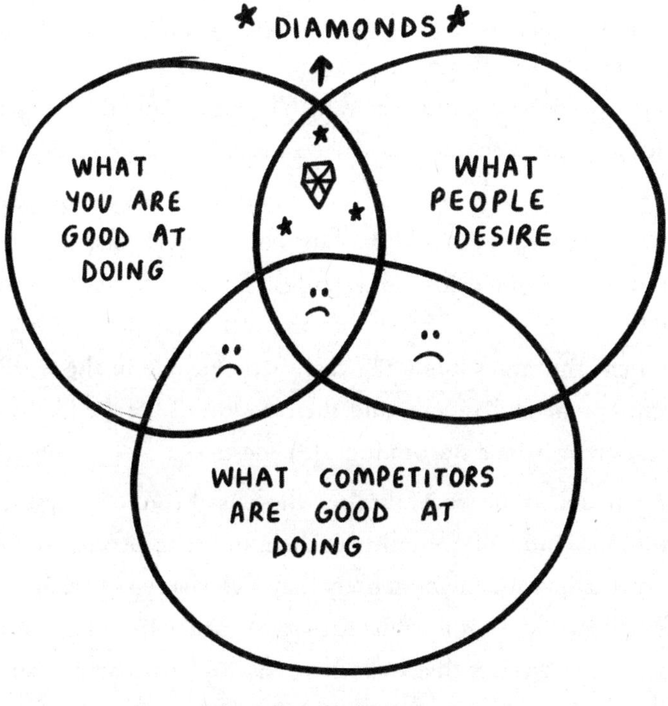

The valley of value creation

Scott Adams, the cartoon Dilbert's creator, gave excellent career advice on his blog. He recommends mastering multiple skills until no one else has the mix that you have. That's great advice.

The same applies to startups too—the only way to succeed in the market is if you provide something that's rare and valuable to customers. For example, Facebook succeeded because it fulfilled the desire of college students to know who from their class is available for dating (the valuable part). Before Facebook, social networks weren't limited to a particular college, making it difficult to find people in your class who are looking for a relationship. By limiting signups initially to just Harvard University, Facebook created the ultimate destination for dating. No other social network did this at that point in time, so Facebook provided a unique value to people (the rare part). If Facebook did only the valuable part or only the rare part, it would have not succeeded. A startup needs both to succeed.

A fatal but common mistake that entrepreneurs make is misjudging what makes something valuable. Many entrepreneurs start companies around their own passions and desires. When it comes to startups, scratching your own itch assumes that other people also have the same itch. But that's rarely the case. Most people in the world are not entrepreneurs like you, and their desires in life are likely to be very different from a startup founders' desires.

If you look at the world through the lens of your own desires and frustrations, you will overestimate the number of people who share your worldview and how intensely they feel what you feel. So, if you don't understand what is valuable to *others*, you will end up building products and services that nobody needs. To have a shot at success, build things that people (not you) want.

Once you successfully identify a broadly shared desire or frustration, *another costly mistake you might make is to ignore how such desires or frustrations are currently being serviced.* If existing options are doing a good-enough job in fulfilling such needs, your odds of success in the market decrease substantially.

Why would customers switch from the tried and tested options to yours, which is unknown to them? People—you, me, everyone else—are lazy.

Net net, *startup success requires identifying specific desires of people that others haven't yet figured out.* Doing this is difficult. You may either successfully identify what's valuable or you may successfully identify what's rare. But can you identify what's both rare and valuable?

Note that your capabilities are the only thing you are in control of. You can neither change people's priorities, nor what types of competitors exist. But you can definitely change who you are or what you can offer.

While using this framework, it's tempting to ignore reality to justify your gut feelings. If you're intent on deluding yourself, your mind can easily exaggerate the differences of your products from competitors' or misinterpret encouragement from friends as evidence of working on a valuable problem. You might think you've stumbled upon a rare and valuable idea, while in reality, that's your mind deluding you by ignoring the harsh reality.

So, err on the side of being skeptical. Discovering an idea that's rare and valuable is not easy as it requires tremendous insight, iterations and luck, and that's why successful startups are also so rare and valuable.

> **Remember:** the valley of value creation lies at the intersection of what's valuable and what's rare.

BUSINESSES EXIST TO FULFIL HUMAN DESIRES

Human desires have been shaped by millions of years of evolution and, therefore, haven't changed much during the course of history. In fact, the most fundamental desires of food, sex, health and security have remained the same as they were for our hunter–gatherer ancestors. A Homo sapien from 1,00,000 years ago would go for ice-cream over broccoli, just like you would.

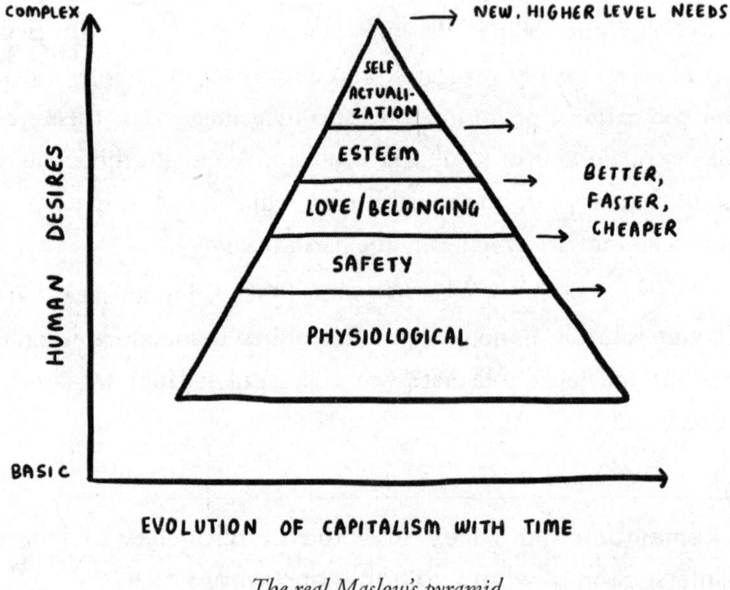

The real Maslow's pyramid

Over time, as culture evolves, new derivative desires emerge to help fulfil our basic ones in a better way. For example, the desire for transportation is derived from the desire for doing business in far-flung areas, which in turn is derived from the desire for profit, which itself is derived from our desire to feel safe by hoarding resources for the rainy days.

You see, there's always a hierarchy of desires and no matter how novel a desire may appear (say the desire to livestream on YouTube), it is ultimately in service of a fundamental desire that's shaped by evolution (in YouTube's case, it is to be entertaining or appear desirable with the aim of improving status and prestige).

Startups displace old companies only because people are forever looking to fulfil their desires in a better way than before. We are perennially dissatisfied, and capitalism is a system that tirelessly works to satisfy us through technology and creativity.

Despite our basic desires remaining the same, we have always been welcoming of better ways to fulfil them. This drives ways we opt for to become faster, cheaper, more entertaining, of higher quality, while taking lesser time, cost or effort. That's the magic of capitalism.

This idea of what remains the same and what changes is captured well by Jeff Bezos in his 2016 letter to Amazon shareholders:

> Customers are always beautifully, wonderfully dissatisfied, even when they report being happy and business is great. Even when they don't yet know it, customers want something better, and your desire to delight customers will *drive you to invent* on their behalf. [emphasis mine]

A similar insight comes from his answer to what will change in the next ten years, to which he replied:[1]

> I very frequently get the question: 'What's going to change in the next 10 years?' And that is a very interesting question; it's a very common one. I almost never get the question: 'What's not going to change in the next 10 years?' And I submit to you that that second question is actually the more important of the two — because *you can build a business strategy around the things that are stable in time* … [I]n our retail business, we know that customers want low prices, and I know that's going to be true 10 years from now. They want fast delivery; they want vast selection. [emphasis mine]

What fuels capitalism is not the shiny new thing but the old one done in a better way.

> **Remember:** always ask yourself what human desire is your business fulfilling, and how can you fulfil it better, cheaper and faster than the current alternatives?

EVIDENCE OF DESIRE IS IN PEOPLE'S BEHAVIOUR (AND NOT IN WHAT THEY SAY)

Many people say they want to quit smoking or reduce their alcohol intake.

Yet the same evening they find themselves smoking or drinking again. How many times have your friends told you that they want to get fitter, but then you discover them ordering a large, cheesy pizza?

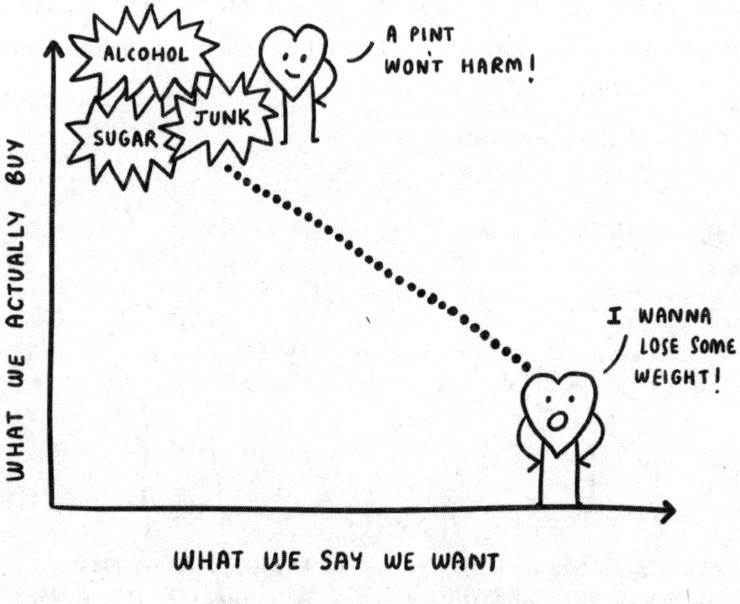

The deluded customer

We, humans, are notorious for saying something but doing something else. This tendency is troublesome for entrepreneurs because when people express their desire for something, it's a mistake to take that on its face value.

What we tell others is driven by our desire to appear as nice, visionary and thoughtful. So, we usually end up saying all the right-sounding stuff. We're angels in our thoughts, but when it comes to our actions, we're driven by our more primal fears and desires (think: love, money, security, fame, sugar).

You, the entrepreneur, need to deeply understand this inconsistency between what we say and what we do.

As an entrepreneur, the biggest mistake you can make is to believe potential customers when they say they either like or dislike your idea.

A fantastic example of this is Spirit Airlines. It's the most hated airline in the US, but it is also the most profitable. How can that be? Clearly, for the vast majority of air travellers, no matter what they say online, the desire to save money while travelling is more important than their desire for comfort.

Customers vote with their wallets because words are cheap, while money is expensive.

So, don't ask people what they want. Most won't tell you the truth about their actual behaviour because they themselves don't know about it until they're ready to act. *To spot strong human desires, instead of asking people, watch what they do and what sort of products and services they pay money for.*

> **Remember:** behaviour, not words, is the real evidence of desire.

NO MARKET IS EVER DONE

Our desires usually remain the same, but how we fulfil them keeps on changing. For example, the desire to have good oral hygiene can be fulfilled in multiple ways: toothbrushes or mouthwash. Even crunchy foods like carrots that help clean the mouth as we chew on them (and some people use them).

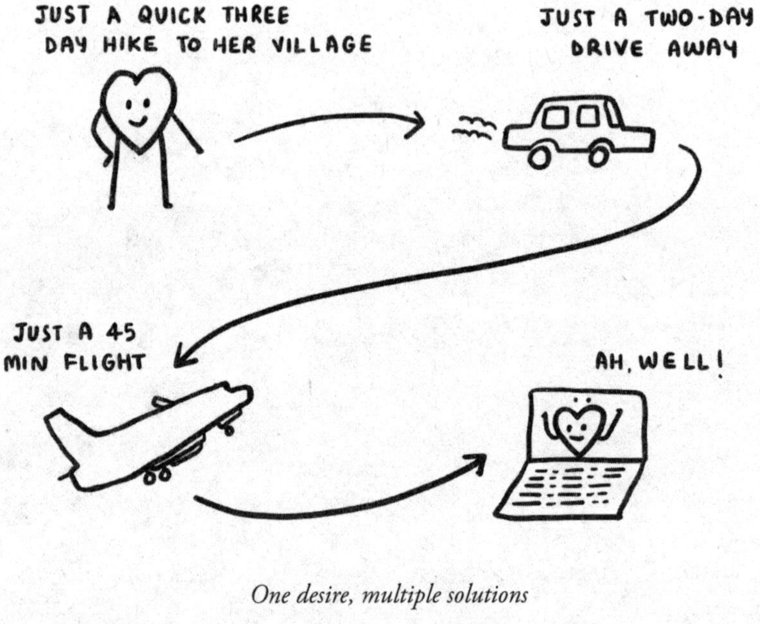

One desire, multiple solutions

Smart entrepreneurs know that what people care about is their desires and not how they're currently fulfilling them. If a better way to fulfil their desire—also known as 'jobs' in the popular 'jobs-to-be-done' framework for building products—comes along, they'll switch to it in a jiffy. This is why innovative startups take over entrenched incumbents. People really have no loyalty to solutions.

Since there are always multiple ways of cleaning the mouth, an established toothbrush company doesn't just compete with other toothbrush companies. It also has to compete with all the alternative ways of keeping good oral hygiene (such as mouthwash or people chewing carrots).

This is good news for entrepreneurs because it means no market is ever done. Even before toothbrushes came along, people cared for their oral hygiene and even after toothbrushes are long gone, people will still care for their oral hygiene.

Since desires always remain, there's always an opening for better solutions to replace the old ones.

Let's look at a few more examples. Our desire for music has always remained but the methods for fulfilling that desire have evolved from live orchestra, vinyl records, cassettes, CDs, MP3 players, to newer solutions now such as Spotify. Similarly, our desire for finding information has also always remained but what has changed is that we've stopped going to libraries or looking at Yellow Pages and have started Googling. Tomorrow, even Googling can stop but our thirst for finding information will never go away. (Hello, ChatGPT?)

Entrepreneurs are fond of saying that their solutions are unique in the market and hence they have no competitors. That's not true. People do not sit idle waiting for a perfect solution to arrive in the market. They're always using something or the other to fulfil their desires. If nothing ready-made exists, they'll look for a solution (for example, in Excel spreadsheets). You may not identify a particular product as a competitor as it's hacky or suboptimal, but it's there and people use it. The first-ever search engine really did compete with the Yellow Pages because that's what people were using to find information.

So, no matter how unique, all new things compete with old things.

As an entrepreneur, you need to have clarity on what human desire are you trying to fulfil and what existing alternatives are available to the customer to fulfil that desire. Even though CRM software and Microsoft Excel seem to be serving different markets, from the lens of desires, they compete head-on-head because both fulfil the same desire of business owners to keep track of their customers.

> **Remember:** solutions come and go, but desires always remain.

PART 2

GETTING READY FOR SUCCESS

SERVE THE DISSATISFIED MINORITY FIRST

Isn't it surprising that startups exist at all? The world is and has always been full of established businesses offering solid products. Consumers also have established patterns of behaviours—they buy

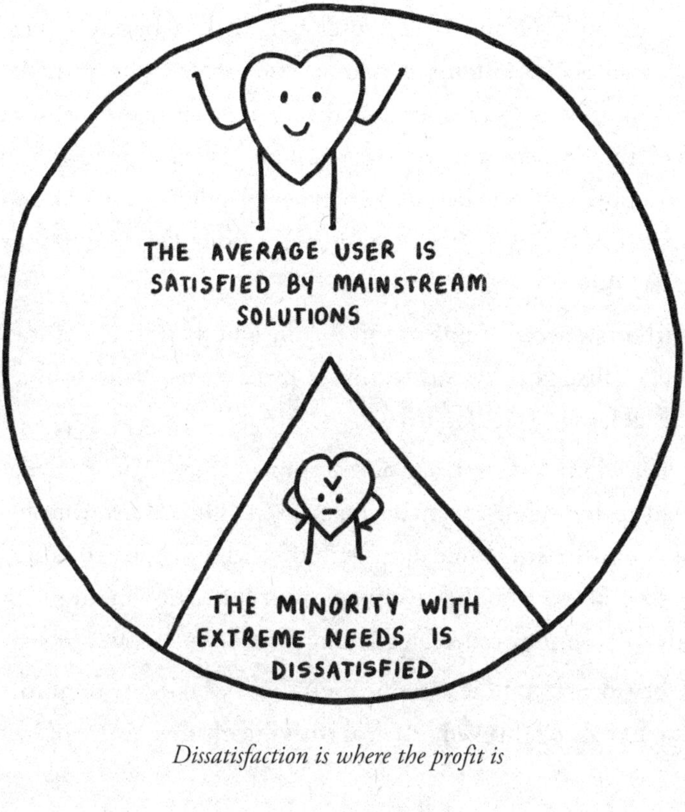

Dissatisfaction is where the profit is

things they've always bought from the places they always shop at. We don't experiment much, and when we do, we tend to de-risk and go for what's popular and that's often a product from an established business.

HOW CAN A STARTUP THEN SUCCEED?

When you study cases of startups that have succeeded in the past, one pattern clearly emerges: They tend to enter a market focused on the extreme user, not the mainstream one. The extreme user's needs are so different from the mainstream one's and are so few that the established companies end up ignoring them.

An example of an extreme user would be a business traveller arriving in a city last minute for a conference. The mainstream user books hotels in advance, but this one makes plans last minute. Unlike the mainstream, the last-minute traveller doesn't want a fancy lobby, coffee machine, two types of pillows, and so on. All this person wants is a place to crash, and Airbnb emerged to provide precisely this.

Airbnb's success came from the insight that the last-minute traveller's first priority was to find a place to safely sleep in a city where all hotels were booked.

Uber's initial days make for a similar story. The taxi market catered to two kinds of mainstream users: One, those who hailed a cab from the street but didn't mind waiting if they couldn't hail one. Two, those who didn't want to wait but didn't mind planning in advance, so they called a taxi company to send a cab.

Uber focused on the extreme user: those who didn't want to plan ahead, but also didn't want to deal with the inconvenience of hailing a cab. Such users were okay paying some premium for it. And that's what Uber launched in 2013 with their first product—Uber Black—where a taxi for your destination appears at your doorstep with a single click.

It's not worthwhile for startups to focus on mainstream needs because: One, the mainstream consumer is already satisfied with existing offerings and won't easily switch to yours. Two, even if you manage to convince some mainstream users to use your offering, established companies will fight aggressively to retain this market share by copying your products or through advertising and promotions.

So, as a startup, you should enter into a market focused on users with extreme needs. Such users have a burning pain that only your customized offering can cure uniquely.

Once you satisfy the extreme user, you can either march slowly towards the mainstream or expect the mainstream market to evolve a desire towards extremities (which is what is happening for Airbnb as more and more people like staying in cosy homes, not hotels).

Remember: as a startup, you need to focus on those who're currently most dissatisfied. Often, they're the users with extreme desires that the mainstream finds unprofitable to fulfil.

PRODUCTS CAN'T CREATE DESIRES, THEY ONLY SATISFY THEM

Motivation is a mysterious thing. Some are motivated to wake up at 5 a.m. every day, while others can't get up unless their alarm rings multiple times and it's getting late for work. Some run 5K daily, while others hate walking even 100 metres.

Why does this happen?

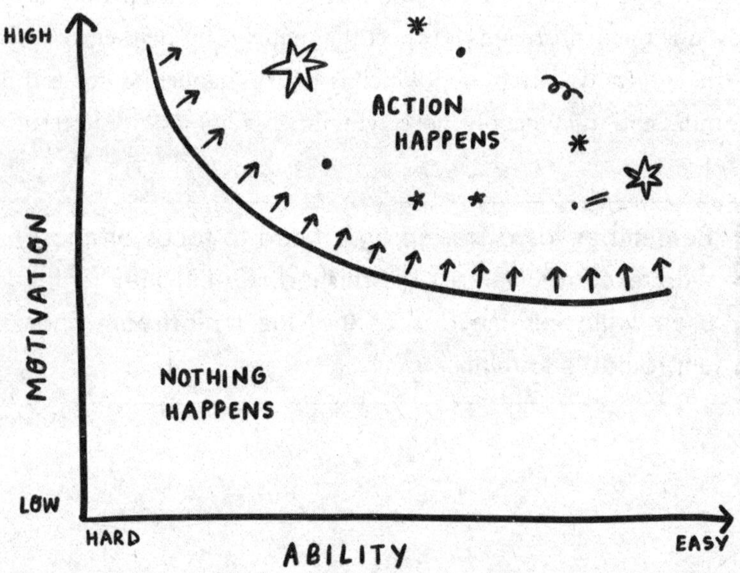

Make it compelling and then make it easy

This simply means that different people have a dramatically different life context. People's current motivations are a function of their life history and present circumstances.

Some people are book lovers because they grew up in households full of books. Same is true for many other behaviours. Maybe someone is into fitness because their friends got them into it, or maybe they faced a health crisis.

Whatever the case may be, motivating people to exhibit a dramatically new desire is close to impossible. People do evolve their desires over time (that is, they pick up and try new things all the time) but that is often because of their social circle, and not because your product exists.

The field of behavioural change is littered with failure, with even doctors unable to motivate patients with severe heart conditions to start exercising or give up on their oily diets.

So, what hope do you, the no-name startup, have in having people switch their current priorities?

Instead of hoping to create a desire in people, what you should do instead is to help them fulfil their desires efficiently. Make it easier, faster, cheaper for people to do what they're already motivated to do.

Note that I wrote what *they're already doing*, and not what they *say* they want to do. This is because what people say and what they do is different. We say we want to get fit, but what we *really* want is a bag of chips.

> **Remember:** if people aren't already exhibiting a desire that your product depends upon, you're dead on arrival.

DON'T MAKE PEOPLE WORK HARDER THAN THEY'RE USED TO

To make money, simplify your customer's life. Help them satisfy their desires in a cheaper, faster and easier way.

Pick any successful product, and it will be immediately obvious how they made something easier. Tinder? Swipe to find love (vs earlier—go through long profiles, most of which were uninteresting). Uber? Tap on the icon and you get a taxi on your doorstep (vs

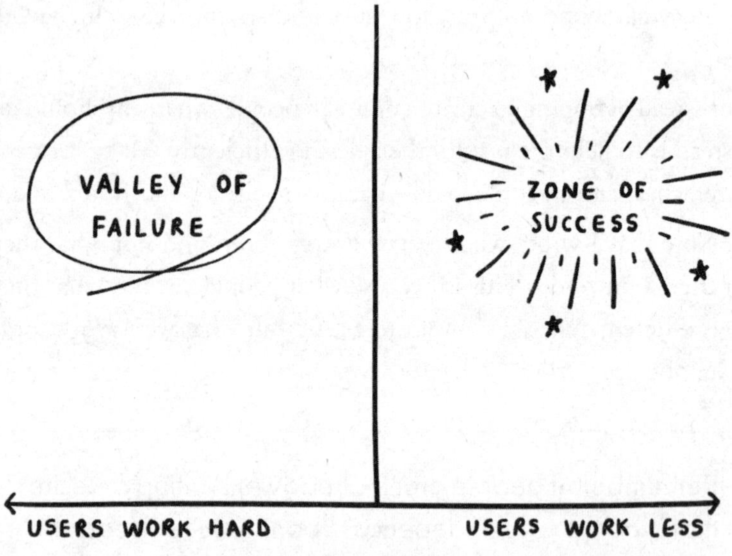

Nobody likes to work hard

earlier—you stand on the street and wait until you find one). Smartphone? Lightweight, full-screen computer in your pocket.

You get the drift?

If business history teaches us anything, it is that whenever a product eliminates effort, people flock to it.

It may appear that some products defy this rule. For example, how do you explain people standing in queues to buy new gadgets or a new Harry Potter book? The answer here is that only early adopters put in this effort and that they're *used to* jumping through the hoops to be the first one to own a product. The key term here is 'used to', which means a product isn't making anyone work harder than before.

Ultimately, all consumers are making a rational decision: what effort does a product demand and what reward are they expected to get from that effort. Effort can be money, cognitive effort, physical effort, reputation or time. Reward is what people are motivated to get. It could be status, love, taxi, hotel or a million other things we humans find rewarding.

Note that your ability to impact motivation is much lesser than your ability to reduce effort.

As an example, imagine two taxi companies. One focuses on effort: tap the icon and you get a taxi at your doorstep. The other focuses on reward: The taxi driver will tell you entertaining stories, but you have to walk to the taxi stand and wait until one for-hire comes along. Which one would you prefer?

The reason Uber got successful is because overwhelmingly, people prefer reduction in effort over rewards. Sure, people like rewarding experiences but typically won't work harder than they're used to.

So, unless you're in the entertainment business where the whole point is to create a rewarding experience, focus on making people work less hard than before.

PS: You can make people work harder, but only if you pay them. People slog through jobs only because they're getting paid. But a startup's job is to get people to pay, and not to pay them.

> **Remember**: people pay when you simplify their life (or when you dazzle them, but dazzling is hard).

SUCCESSFUL PRODUCTS SATISFY CORE MOTIVATIONS EFFORTLESSLY

There are only a handful of core motivations shared by all humans. The specific list is debatable but it likely includes the desire to have higher status, finding love/sex, making more money or being entertained.

These core motivations lead to downstream, derivative motivations. For example, higher status leads to desire for beauty, which for some people may lead to the desire for nose rings.

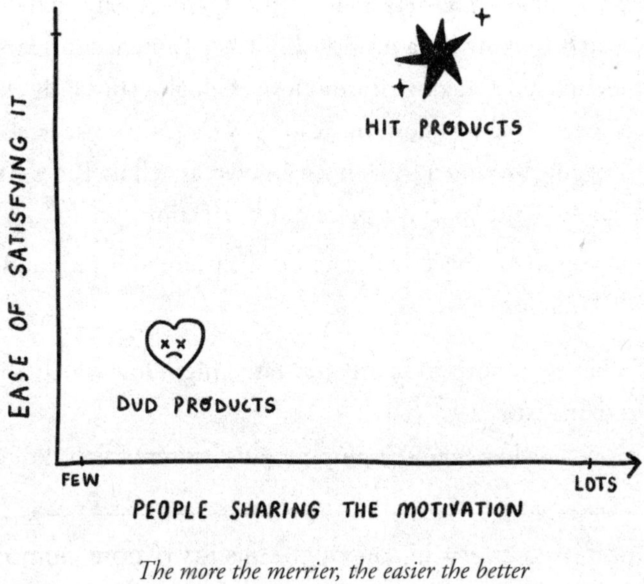

The more the merrier, the easier the better

Products can be successful by simplifying desires at any level—either core or derivative. But the scale of success depends on how core is the motivation being targeted by a product. Everything else being equal, a nose ring company will have a smaller market than a dating app company (which solves for a core motivation: of finding a mate).

But everything else isn't often equal. Your ability to offer a radically better alternative to existing offerings may be different for different levels of motivations. (For example, you can't think of ways to improve upon dating apps but can have a dramatically good idea for improving upon nose rings).

When I say 'improving', I mean requiring less effort from customers than before while delivering an equal or more rewarding experience. If you observe hit products around you (Facebook, LinkedIn, Google, iPhone, Salesforce), all of them attacked a core human desire shared universally and innovated on satisfying it in a radically simpler way than before. Facebook—easily know who around you is looking for a relationship (they launched in Harvard, and students have raging hormones). Google—instantly know whatever you want to know (instead of sifting through irrelevant links or lugging around a thick book known as Yellow Pages). Who doesn't have a desire to find a piece of information?

I urge you to do this exercise and dissect more hit products you know of. Think of:

- What core motivation are they targeting? How widely shared is that desire?
- How did they *radically* simplify satisfaction of that desire?

Remember: every hit product satisfies a core human desire.

YOUR JOB IS TO SIGNIFICANTLY INCREASE EFFICIENCY IN SATISFYING DESIRES

Evolution has programmed us humans (and other life forms) to seek more rewards for less effort. This drive for finding ways to get more done with less is deeply ingrained. Our ancestors, who were more efficient, survived tougher times when resources were scarce.

Since efficiency is such a fundamental desire, it drives much of the consumer behaviour. Why do things become cheaper over time? Because humans would prefer paying less for the same thing if they could. This is painfully obvious.

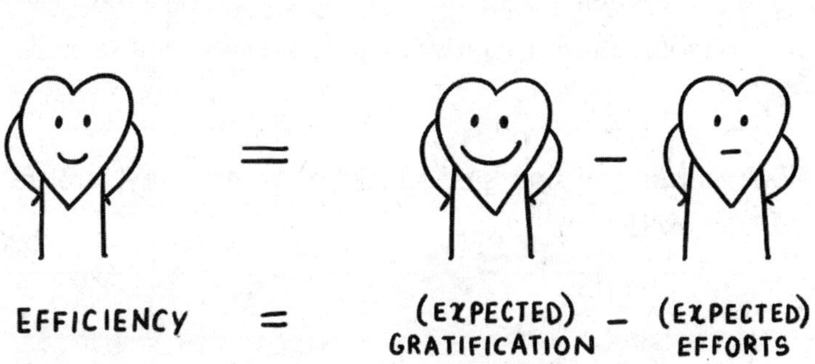

All we want in life is efficiency

Less obvious is that the only way to achieve success with new products is to deliver significantly more efficiency to customers than *all* the current alternatives they're currently using.

To illustrate this idea, consider Uber. Why did it succeed? It dramatically lowered the effort to get a cab as compared to the old ways. Why did PayPal succeed? It dramatically lowered the hassle it required to send money to distant people (cross-border) while also providing mild gratisfaction (the $10 you got on signup in the early days). Why did Gmail succeed? It dramatically increased gratification by offering a 1 GB inbox space while everyone else was offering 10 MB.

Note that I mention expected gratification and expected effort to underscore the subjective nature of these assessments. Gratification (or reward) and the effort is in the customer's head, and they're always making a decision about whether they're going to get more from a product (or experience) than they put into it.

Gratification can be anything people value—status, food, love, safety, money, mastery, autonomy.

Effort is anything people consider as something they'd rather *not* do. These are often things that require energy/expenditure—pay money, physical effort, cognitive effort, reputation and so on.

> **Remember**: businesses succeed when they create efficiency for customers.

PRODUCT-MARKET FIT REQUIRES DELTA 4 IN EFFICIENCY

Imagine you build a new toothbrush. Maybe one that's fragrant. You're excited about it, spent money patenting it. After spending a year, you finally take it out for a pilot. You ask the focus group whether they like it and everyone says yes, they love it—who wouldn't love a toothbrush that smells fantastic, especially when it doesn't cost more than other mass-market options.

Enthused with the feedback, you invest money for its launch, but after an initial tick, it bombs. People aren't buying it. What happened?

Here's what happened.

Your product was an improvement, but that improvement wasn't large enough for people to break their old, habitual ways of purchasing and using whatever they've always done.

Habits exist to save energy. Imagine if each action of ours required deliberate effort. Our brain wouldn't be able to do anything else—when to eat, how to drive, what to eat. All these little decisions would overwhelm us.

$$\Delta = \text{SATISFACTION OF YOUR PRODUCT} \ \underline{\text{MINUS}} \ \text{SATISFACTION OF PREVIOUS SOLUTION} \geq 4$$

Is your product Delta 4?

This is why it's useful to imagine humans as automations—they'll continue doing whatever they're used to doing unless something comes along that promises to increase efficiency in their life to an extent that makes it worthwhile to break old habits.

Notice how even the decision to try new products is driven by efficiency. Since breaking an established routine (which includes using current products) is effortful and hence a cost, the expected gratification from new products has to be large enough for people to take action.

How to quantify if your product is good enough that people will be willing to break their old habits?

There are multiple ways to do that. One is what Kunal Shah names Delta 4.[1] He recommends entrepreneurs ask people to rate their satisfaction on a scale of 1–10 for both, the existing products and the new product. If the difference in rating is ≥4 favouring your product, you have a shot at breaking old habits.

Another method is to give your product to people and ask how disappointed they would be if the product were taken away from them. Sean Ellis recommends that if ≥ 40% of people say that they'll be very disappointed if your product is taken away, you have a product-market fit (PMF).[2]

All such benchmarks are ultimately a rough heuristic. The core message is that products hit PMF when one, people can't go back to the old ways once they have used your new product, and two, they can't stop telling their friends about your new product they've been using.

> **Remember:** people will only change their behaviour if you offer them a significant (not incremental) increase in satisfaction over old ways.

FORGET ABOUT MARKET SIZE, FOCUS ON EFFICIENCY INSTEAD

Many entrepreneurs obsess over the market size. It's a useless exercise because what you should be interested in is not the current market size of your product but its *potential* market size. You should be answering not how many widgets are sold today, but how many of the new, improved widget that you're developing can be sold in future.

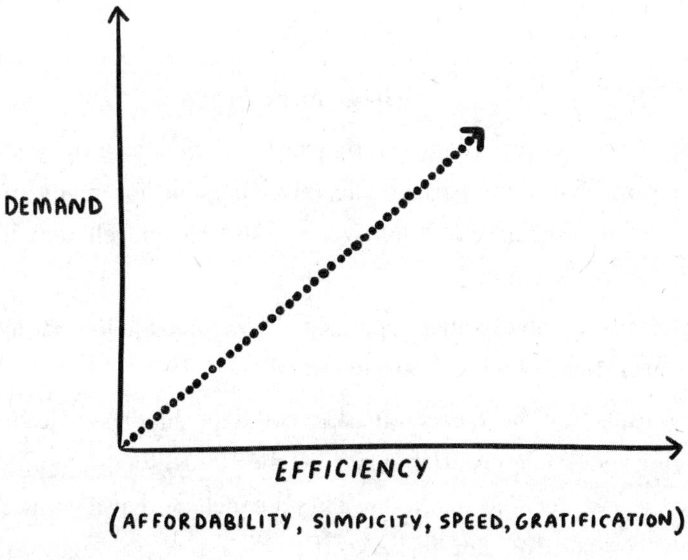

Demand rises when you make things efficient

And, how do you figure that out?

You can't estimate it without answering how large of an improvement your product is going to make.

If your product's improvement over current solutions is marginal, it won't change anything.

(By the way, why work on something that's essentially similar to what already exists? A startup's top job is to discover new efficiencies in the world and deliver them to people.)

So, let's assume that you've increased efficiency through your product (that is, lowered the cost or effort significantly, made it easier or more gratifying to use). You'd obviously attract customers who're using existing, less-efficient products. But, interestingly, you'll also expand the market dramatically because higher efficiency now makes it worthwhile for previously non-customers to start desiring your product.

Perhaps, an example would help. Before aeroplanes were invented, international travel typically happened through steamer ships that took weeks of time investment for travel.

So, when aeroplanes arrived, they not only took over the market share from ships, they also made travel possible for many more people who didn't have multiple weeks to spare for travelling (which is what ships demanded).

Do you see how planes expanded the market for international travel by providing a breakthrough in efficiency?

Focusing on the current market could be highly misleading. Imagine an aeroplane entrepreneur (in the 1920s) focusing on how large the steamer ship market is. They'd conclude that it's tiny and highly competitive, not realizing that their breakthrough would translate into market expansion.

As another example, Duolingo—a popular language learning app—reported that 80 per cent of its users weren't actively trying to learn a language before trying the app. This is not because people aren't interested in learning foreign languages. The existence of a small population that goes through expensive offerings (such as live classes) is proof that the human desire to learn languages is there. But it's so costly and effort-intensive that most people don't bother. Duolingo simplified access to languages radically and expanded the market massively.

By the way, this closely resembles the Jevons paradox—an empirical observation that when cars become more fuel-efficient, the total volume of fuel consumption increases because people start driving more.

It's the eternal truth—we humans always want more for less!

> **Remember:** obsess over whether you have a breakthrough, not how big the market is.

PART 3

DISCOVERING YOUR EDGE

SEARCH FOR MARKET-PRODUCT FIT, NOT PRODUCT-MARKET FIT

It's near impossible for a product to create a new desire in customers all by itself. *No single product creates a market.* What usually happens is that multiple trends evolve to create market opportunities. Perhaps, there has been a tech breakthrough, incomes are rising, or people aren't getting married anymore.

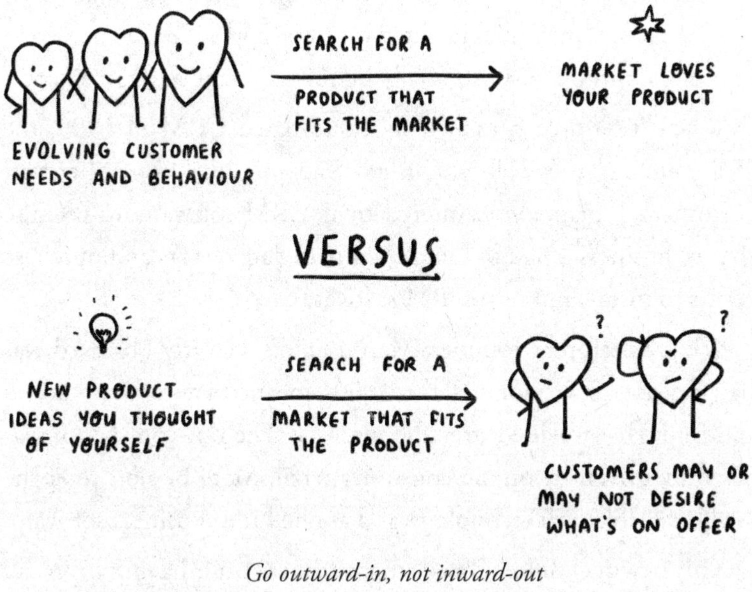

Go outward-in, not inward-out

There are so many of these big changes happening in the world that the million dollar question begs itself: how do you spot viable startup opportunities within these trends?

One good way to answer the question is to *look for instances where customers are innovating by themselves* by modifying or reimagining existing products.

Innovative customers have guided entrepreneurs throughout history—from lugging big stereo systems, which led to the inspiration for portable music players, to scooting their cars off the paved road, which led to the inspiration for SUVs.

Figuring out *why* customers are doing what they're doing can provide deep insights into their desires. Maybe not all people want cars to satisfy their desire to go from point A to point B. Maybe some want cars to satisfy their desire for adventure?

Take a hard look at what new tech is available today that wasn't possible before; then imagine how it can be applied to fulfil existing customer desires in a substantially better way than the status quo.

When Salesforce launched its cloud-based CRM in 1999, the CRM industry was well-established with offerings from Microsoft and other IT giants who offered their CRM software on-premise (that is, businesses had to build their own data servers and purchase servers to install and host CRM software).

What Salesforce's founder, Marc Benioff, cleverly observed was that the dot-com boom of the 1990s meant that software access could now be provided over the internet. The dot-com boom was primarily driven by online consumer retail. Marc Benioff took the newly available web technology and applied it to business software.

This new technology freed up customers from having to install their own servers, which meant that a much wider set of businesses could now use a CRM. Notice how this efficiency in CRM hosting expanded the market as many more businesses, who previously couldn't afford to buy servers for CRM, could now use hosted CRM.

Also note that Salesforce didn't create the desire for CRM—managing customer databases is a human need as old as businesses. What they did was to take an upcoming technology (cloud computing) and apply it to serve the same old customer desire in a radically cheaper, better and faster way.

It's risky to get excited about an idea first and then go about researching the market. The excitement of an idea will cloud your judgement and inevitably lead you to find confirmatory evidence for it while rejecting all the contradicting evidence. You may think you're objective but unless you've had special training as a market researcher or you've failed and learned by yourself many times, you'll keep falling into confirmation bias towards your pre-existing ideas during research.

Therefore, instead of starting with an idea and then doing research, it's much better to *start with a blank slate and start observing customer behaviour and trends.* Sooner or later, you'll find yourself full of bright ideas that are grounded in truth. Such market-first ideas have much higher success odds than product-first ideas, which may or may not address an unfilled customer desire.

Remember: shoot for market-product fit, not product-market fit.

WHAT'S POSSIBLE NOW THAT WASN'T POSSIBLE BEFORE?

Markets are usually co-created by multiple competitors offering to satisfy a particular customer desire. Even the markets that seem to be dominated by one company usually have multiple credible competitors—Google has Bing and DuckDuckGo and Facebook has Twitter, TikTok and Snapchat.

Multiple competitors exist because the first company to launch a product is rarely a home run in terms of getting the market-product fit right.

The usual evolution of a market goes something like this.

First, a few startups or big companies launch innovative products that customers aren't yet ready to adopt because what's offered is often too unfamiliar, costly or inconvenient. Think of that awkward first-generation product in any category that most customers feel weirded out by.

However, not all customers reject innovations. Early adopters love to try the new. And if a product succeeds with early adopters (and many don't because nobody wanted it in the first place), the first line of evidence emerges that there's an unfulfilled desire in the mass market.

But many early entrants struggle because they keep focused on early adopters for long. Early adopters are not only a small market

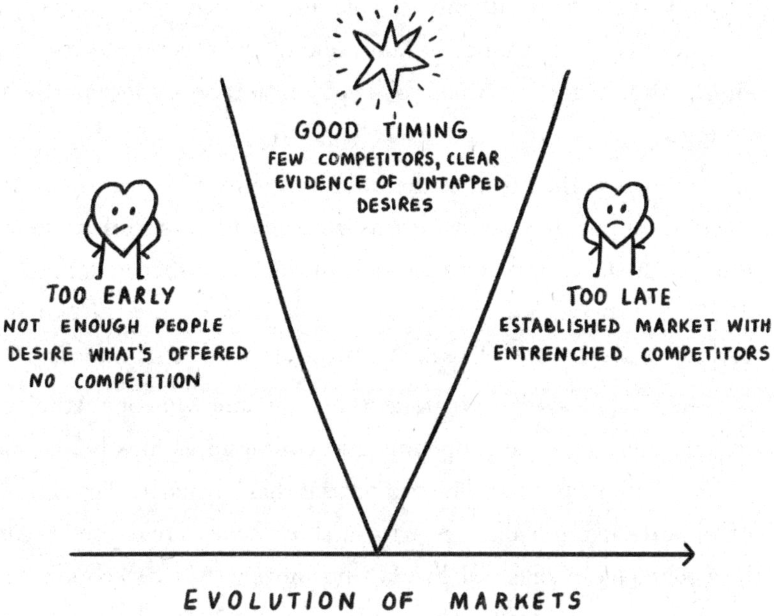

The window of startup opportunity

but often overwhelm the company with their feedback and non-stop demands. At this stage, a smart entrepreneur should observe and learn from the limited but certain success of innovations with early adopters. Study what they got right, and what they got wrong. Think of electric cars before Tesla. What made early adopters rave about electric cars? Why did the mainstream not adopt it?

After early experiments by multiple companies in trying to kickstart a market, there's a narrow window when the timing is just right for a good solution that's affordable, fast and convenient for the mass market. The window to penetrate the mass market is narrow because the hype from awkward early experiments tempts many players to jump into the game with their own takes on the product. And, sooner or later, one of them is bound to get it right. After Dogpile, Altavista, Lycos and Yahoo, Google finally emerged.

And hence, the business that dominates the market is often not the pioneer but the one that learns from all early experiments being done to finally get it right enough to penetrate the mass market. Think Facebook, not MySpace. Think iPhone, not Blackberry. History is littered with late movers overtaking the first movers.

The good news for entrepreneurs is that windows of opportunities for startups always keep opening and closing in various markets at different points in time. The bad news is that any particular window of opportunity remains open for a short time. Therefore, *timing* in a market can make or break a business. Launch too soon and customers reject it for being too unfamiliar, and launch too late and the market is already well-established.

Both, having no competitors or having too many competitors is a clear sign of wrong timing. Don't build things nobody wants. And don't build things that competitors are already fulfilling. Capitalism rewards rare and valuable.

> **Remember:** be an early mover, but don't be a first mover, as the lack of competition most likely signifies a lack of genuine customer desire.

WHAT ARE YOU BETTING ON: CULTURE OR TECH?

There are two ways an entrepreneur can fail: one, launch a product that nobody desires; two, launch a product that people desire but it has no significant advantage over established competitors (hence, you give no strong reason for a customer to switch away).

These two failure modes have their analogous success modes: one, a culture-led startup success, where a new desire is discovered and

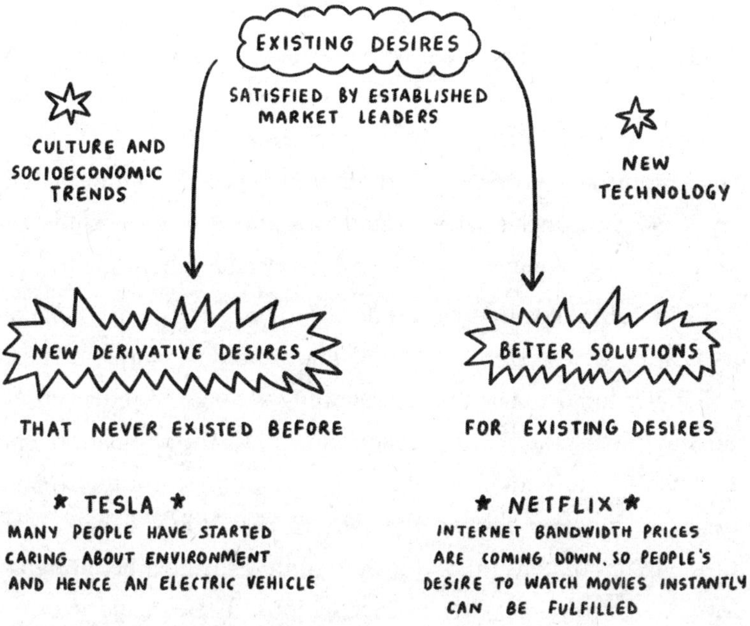

The culture-tech spectrum for startups

fulfilled; a technology-led startup success, where new technology is used to fulfill an existing desire.

Startups are, at the very core, an arbitrage of insight. What are you, dear entrepreneur, betting on that others are not fully realizing?

Are you betting on culture, expecting a nascent demand to become mainstream? Or, are you betting on technology, expecting it to become massively cheaper, faster, better in near term?

CULTURE BETS

Sometimes an entrepreneur is able to observe a pattern of new derivative desires that didn't exist before. This is Elon Musk betting on electric vehicles before all major car makers. Spotting such trends is tricky because, initially, they can be mistaken either as fads or insignificant.

However, an entrepreneur who has good observation skills is able to connect the dots from diverse sources to grow her conviction about a cultural shift just when the market is ripe for it. This is why keeping an eye on early signs of growth in VC-funding activity, new-product launches, new regulations and new careers/jobs is a great way to get a sense of which cultural trends are imminent.

New cultural and socio-economic trends create new markets by creating new desires in people. The simplest example of this is banking or finance startups in developing nations. Founders of such startups understand that as an economy grows, the population tends to consume more and, therefore, the desire for consumer finance products will naturally emerge. Notice that this is a bet on the future desires of consumers, but it is an informed bet because that's how the story has played in other nations. There's solid data that demand for banking grows as GDP does. The need for consumer finance always grows as an economy develops. This happened in the

US and other western countries, and now it is happening in India and China, and soon it'll happen in Africa.

Another example of culture-led startups is the ever-growing number of startups around the idea of sharing and renting economy because the success of Uber and Airbnb has softened consumers into trusting strangers. This cultural change led to hundreds of other successful startups that are enabling, among many other services, sharing dog-walking (Rover, Petbnb) and car-parking (JustPark, ParkAmigo). Such companies are not using new technology. Rather, they're using the existing technology and shifts in culture to offer a cheaper and more convenient solution to age-old desires of dog-walking and parking.

Before Airbnb and Uber, trusting strangers was tough. Now, culture has evolved for us to take that for granted.

Established competitors are usually focused on their existing market, which often is built to serve well-established desires. Hence, a culture-led startup often has a wide blue ocean of newly emerging derivative desires to fulfil. And they can often do it cheaply because such startups typically don't need to innovate on technology as they can assemble a solution using pre-existing technology.

BETTING ON TECHNOLOGY

New innovations can substantially improve upon solutions offered by existing players. Think how GPS in smartphones enabled the disruption of traditional maps. The reason technology-led startups succeed is because new technology can help make a new product that's substantially cheaper, better or faster than existing products. And customers love making progress on those dimensions. Tech is a big lever in creating Delta 4 in efficiencies.

Clayton Christensen called this process disruption and suggested that the reason entrenched competitors ignore startups with innovative technology is because initially, technology-led startups do not have a fully built solution for the entire market.[1] New technology often looks like a gimmick in the early days and by the time established players realize the full potential, it's already too late and a startup has gotten the escape velocity it needs. Think how everyone ignores GPT-2 as a toy, until GPT-3 and then ChatGPT took over in a big way.

A classic example of a technology-led startup is Google. Their key innovation was PageRank, using which they offered demonstrably better search results and beat other established players, such as Yahoo and AltaVista, at that time. Another successful technology-led product was the iPhone, which launched in 2007 with an amazing touchscreen, thus providing for a much more natural way of interacting with the phone, and paved the way for phones replacing desktops as our primary computing devices.

CULTURE-TECH SPECTRUM OF TRENDS: A CONTINUUM

In reality, no successful startup is either only culture-led or only technology-led. Usually, there's a mix of both elements in successful startups. For example, Uber realized that people increasingly have internet and GPS-enabled phones and have developed a comfort with transacting online (a cultural trend). So, they combined this insight with technology innovations to produce a significantly better way to fulfil the two pre-existing desires: faster taxi access to consumers and faster customer access to taxi-drivers.

> **Remember:** the best startup ideas capitalize on both emerging cultural trends and emerging technology.

DEFINE YOUR MARKET AS NARROWLY AS POSSIBLE

It's common for entrepreneurs to cast a wide net early on and imagine their market to be huge. The logic goes something like this: if the market is worth a hundred billion dollars, then even if 1 per cent of it is captured, the company will be making a billion dollars.

All this sounds good in theory but in practice, it never works this way.

Why would the market leader—the big fish in the ocean—let you take even 1 per cent of the market? In fact, as soon as your

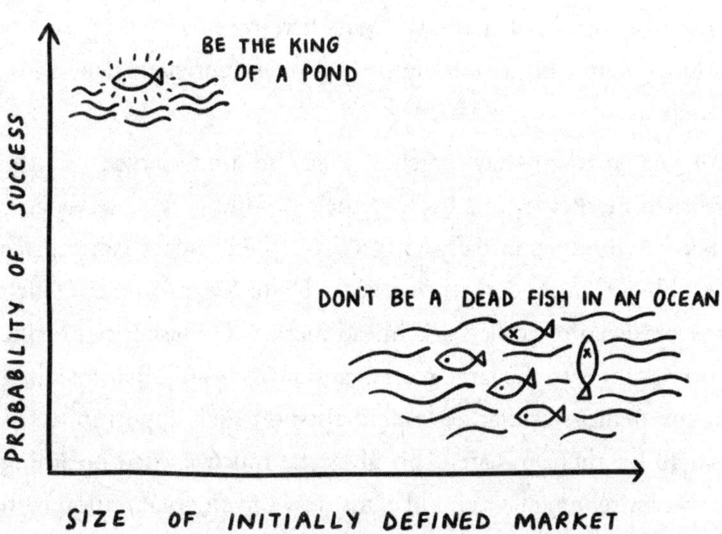

Choose your playground wisely

startup shows first signs of success, the big fish will do whatever it can to crush you and snatch whatever market share you may have won by that time.

In his book *Zero to One*, Peter Thiel says that competition is for losers.[1] Instead of competing and trying to be better, you should try to be so different that people don't even club you in the same category.

And how do you do that? Start by defining the initial market as narrowly as possible.

Instead of going top-down in a big market and taking an arbitrary percentage of it, start bottom-up and actually count the number of customers that your startup is uniquely positioned to capture because your product is so much better for them versus what they have now. Facebook's initial customer base was a few thousand Harvard University students. The initial product was a perfect fit just for Harvard University, and therefore displaced the incumbent Myspace in that market pretty soon. Investors like entrepreneurs who show them a big vision, but they love entrepreneurs who show specificity.

All big markets have niches that are underserved by the established market leaders because their products try to serve large markets. A product initially targeted on these niches can replace the established products by providing a Delta 4 improvement. Such niches are also often called beachhead markets because they provide an entry point into the large market and provide an initial shielding from competitors as market leaders discount such opportunities as too small for them to care. This gives the much-needed breathing space for entrepreneurs to build a business and an organization with relative peace.

Beyond providing a laser-sharp product focus, a narrow market also allows for laser-sharp distribution and marketing. Think about it. If the entirety of your potential market is Harvard University students, to get the word out, you can simply stick posters all over the campus. But what if the entire world is your potential user base. Where would you start sticking the posters, and would you have enough posters doing that anyway?

A common fear that entrepreneurs have is that if they define their market narrowly, they'll undershoot and build a small business. This fear is unfounded. A number-one position in any market, no matter how narrow, often translates into a big enough business. Not all businesses have to and can be Google, Apple, Microsoft or Amazon. Such huge businesses are an exception, not the norm. Also, what usually happens is that most businesses keep on using their number-one position in a narrow market to expand into adjacent markets, and hence, always keep on growing at a steady pace.

Ask yourself: would you rather have a high probability for a business that makes money and grows steadily or a dream of a huge business that has low chances of happening? If you want the former, define your market as narrowly as possible.

> **Remember:** it's better to be the king of a niche than a nobody in a vast ocean.

PART 4

BUILDING THINGS THAT SUCCEED

PEOPLE DON'T LIKE USING TECHNOLOGY

A beautiful contrast exists between how an engineer sees the product under development and how a potential user sees it. Engineers often get excited by technology and the number of options of features they can cram in the gadget. However the user sees all this complexity as overwhelming and off-putting.

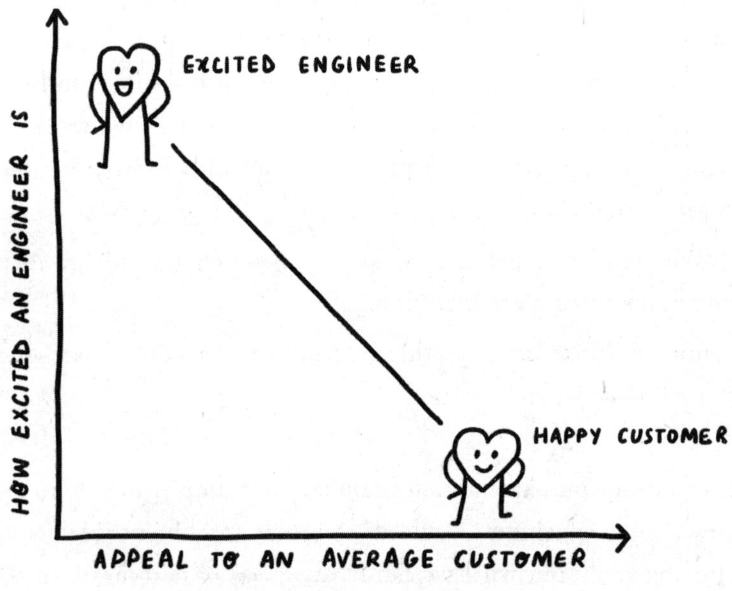

The engineer's fallacy

Whenever you're facing the temptation to add more 'stuff' into your product, remember that users have a life to live, and using your product isn't the highlight of their life. Rather, it's likely a chore.

Products are a means to an end for people, and they want to get to that end as soon as possible, with as little effort as possible. So, if someone wants to go from point A to point B, the most perfect solution would be instant teleportation and not starting the car and driving on the road. People care about their problems, and your solution is only a tool for solving those problems. So make sure you provide them with a convenient tool.

From an engineer's point of view, internal combustion engines are fantastic—making a good engine requires knowledge and application of thermodynamics, acoustics, metals, and so on. Who wouldn't get excited by all that, right? Well, for the busy user, it's a hassle to get into a car, fiddle with the knobs, and then carefully drive to a destination. If the user can avoid all this effort and get an additional hour of life not spent driving, she will switch from driving to teleportation in a jiffy. Everyone will. Even you—the automobile designer.

While engineers get excited by sophisticated technology in a product, potential users want none of it.

James P. Carse captures this perfectly in his book *Finite and Infinite Games*[1] when he writes:

> We do not purchase an automobile, for example, merely to own some machinery. Indeed, it is not machinery we are buying at all, but what we can have by way of it: a means of rapidly carrying us from one location to another, an object of envy for others, protection from the weather. Similarly, a

> radio must cease to exist as equipment and become sound. A perfect radio will draw no attention to itself, will make it seem we are in the very presence of the source of its sounds. Neither do we watch a movie screen nor look at television. We look at what is on television, or in the movie, and become annoyed when the equipment intrudes when the film is unfocused or the speakers hiss.

Apple understands this principle deeply, as evident from the design of the most successful tech product ever: the iPhone. When the iPhone was launched, they took great efforts to remove the stylus, which was the dominant mode of interaction with screens until then (and certainly a fascinating example of technology). Apple innovated on the user experience to make interacting with the iPhone's touchscreen as natural as flipping a magazine.

They knew that nobody wanted to use a phone. What people wanted was to call their friends, write emails and browse the internet. To enable these use cases, they took the latest technology and abstracted away all the complexity from the user. Sure, they could have exposed the variety of configuration options to make the full use of iPhone's underlying technology. But if they did that—like many other phone vendors at that time proudly used to do—they would have killed the iPhone.

Remember: a perfect radio is no radio. It's just music.

EVERYTHING SOPHISTICATED WAS ONCE A PROTOTYPE

There's always a temptation to launch with a killer product, with more features and capabilities than the existing competitors'. It's exciting to build the next Google, the next iPhone or the next SpaceX, isn't it? Moreover, if you don't match features with competitors', how will you kill them?

This temptation to keep building a sophisticated product is dangerous because even the most successful products started simple.

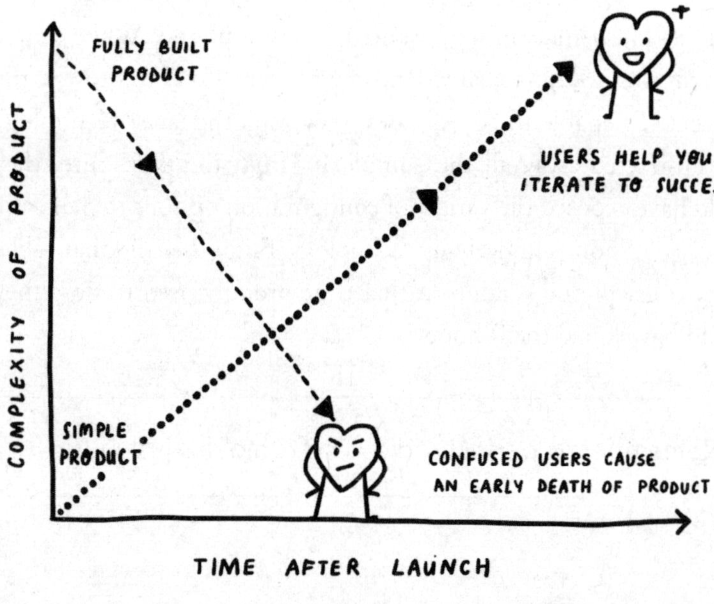

Nothing successful was complex on day one

No product arrives in the market fully fleshed out. A big company behind a successful product has developed its internal capabilities and know-how about various tiny but important details over a long period of time. A startup simply cannot match such capabilities on day one.

Think of your favorite products—from the phone you use to the car you drive. The first version of such products was extremely simple. It's only after thousands of incremental advances that today, these market-dominating products appear so marvellously sophisticated.

Doesn't it then mean that it's impossible to compete in an existing market? You got it!

Yes, it's impossible to beat the existing players if your aim is to compete with them head-on. Mature markets require mature products, and getting there takes time. If you make an attempt to build a sophisticated product in the first go, chances are that you will miss many subtle but important details behind the existing leading products' dominance in the market. Customers never settle for the second best. Why should they?

For a startup, there's also a risk of running out of money or patience during the development of a complex product. On top of this, because the product wasn't iterated in the market, early users are likely to get confused by the strangeness of design.

Lack of frequent feedback may push the product away from what customers want. And once you launch the fully built product, all the feedback on it—a million tiny nuisances and misses—is likely to overwhelm your team.

In short, aiming for a perfect product on day one is a recipe for disaster.

The most famous example of such a disaster is perhaps Apple's first personal computer, Lisa. Its development started in 1978. Steve Jobs wanted it to be perfect before launch, so the launch was delayed multiple times. It finally launched in 1983 with a hefty price tag of $10k.

Lisa was costly because Apple introduced multiple innovations with it on day one—a new OS, a new GUI interface, a new file system and floppy disks. The combination of these innovations translated into a sub-par experience for customers. It was too strange for customers. People like novelty, but not too much of it. Plus, all this innovation that nobody wanted was costly. Hence, selling only 10,000 units, Lisa became Apple's biggest failure, nearly bankrupting them.

What should a product at launch look like? Start with a simple product that excels only on one (or a few) aspects that customers care about, which existing competitors have ignored. Remaining features should be non-existent or extremely basic.

Take Tesla for example. It may seem that in 2003 when they started, the car market was already mature. But they didn't set out to build a general-purpose car. Their first car, Roadster, was a sports car meant for a niche audience. Their strategy was to gain experience in building cars by first aiming at a very specific customer—the one who desired electric sports cars. They didn't try to challenge the automotive industry giants from day one.

Even with that limited ambition, Tesla didn't initially build the technology in-house. They took technical help from a company called AC Propulsion and car manufacturing help from Lotus, a company with seven decades of experience in building cars.[1] Even after all the help, it took Tesla four years—from 2004 to 2008—and multiple prototypes to launch the first version of the Roadster. The Tesla cars that we see today are a result of a very simple first version evolving over a period of time.

All big companies ignore niches, and building an extremely focused product for that niche is a much better strategy than trying to compete with the entire market.

When starting out, aim to be the king of a pond, not a dead fish in the ocean. Once you dominate your pond, you can always aim to dominate another, and much bigger, pond.

Remember: initially, do one thing but do it really well and ignore everything else.

STEAL SUCCESSFUL IDEAS FROM EVERYWHERE

Entrepreneurs are irrationally attached to innovation. In some cases, fresh ideas are absolutely required, but don't forget that your aim is to make money and innovation is just one tool for getting there. Innovation is often costly in terms of time and funding, so in terms of priority, something else should come first—borrowing ideas.

You can actually never 'steal' ideas. They're not like a car, which is either you have it or me. We both can't have the same car. Ideas don't work that way. And the corresponding aversion to exploring ideas pioneered by others can often lead to a significant delay in success (or even failure).

Startups fail for many reasons. Even if you get everything right but err on a specific aspect (say distribution, pricing, onboarding or even the choice of technology), your entire project can fail.

So, you do have to get several things right simultaneously, but that's always significantly more difficult than getting one thing right. Therefore, you should strive to have clarity on what few aspects of the total solution delivered to customers need originality and shamelessly borrow everything else from current best practices.

In short, innovate on a single factor but copy everything else.

By copying what's working for other companies, you can focus on doing just one or a few things really well while resting assured that the remaining parts will probably just work out of the box because they've been tested and proven successful by others.

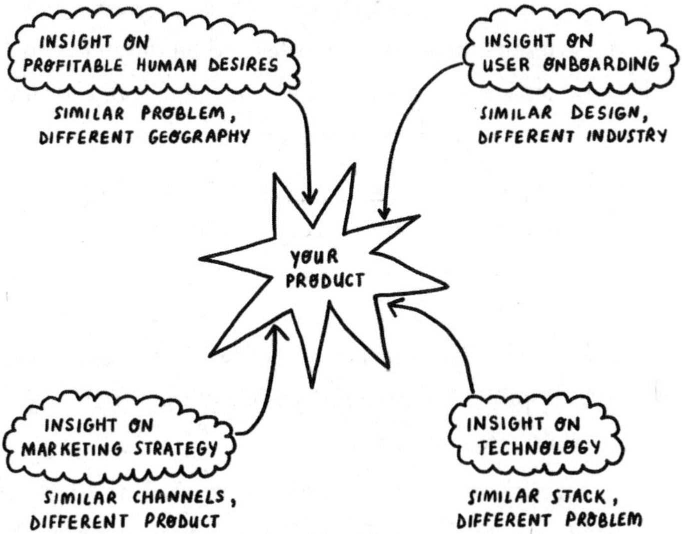

Copying ideas is highly underrated

The most popular example of successful copying is all the Amazon clones that popped up in different geographies. In the US, Amazon successfully demonstrated that people with internet access are willing to buy stuff online. They showed that there was a viable business model in online retail. Entrepreneurs all over the world took this insight and applied it in their respective geographies (Flipkart in India, Zolando in Europe). Actually, what Amazon provided to the world was more than proof of a business model. They innovated on the user interface as well, which is also what Amazon clones copied happily.

But all these clones were not exact copies (if they were, they wouldn't have succeeded since there would be no Delta 4 over Amazon). Different geographies have different challenges that require innovation. Take Flipkart, for example. It's a multi-billion dollar company in India, and its founders learned the model after working at Amazon. Flipkart founders took everything (business model, organization chart, user interface) that Amazon had tested and proved as a starting point, and innovated on only a few variables they thought needed originality: in India, it was lack of wide logistics infrastructure and people having few credit cards.

To make the Amazon model work in India, they pioneered cash on delivery. Flipkart ensured they didn't innovate on things that Amazon proved to just work. Imagine if, along with India-specific innovations, Flipkart also changed the user interface, the organization chart or the business model. With so many undecided variables, a suboptimal solution for any one of them would certainly have meant failure for Flipkart.

Reflect for a moment that you can never copy an idea blindly, you'll always end up adopting the idea to your consent. When you're adapting an idea, try to figure out why it works in the first place. Perhaps the idea depends on some non-obvious detail that you missed?

For example, getting inspired by the iPhone's App Store, many TV manufacturers launched their own app stores. None of them got any traction because the important detail that was lost was the context in which a phone is used. Unlike TV, which is stationary at home, a mobile phone is in a person's pocket. Apps on mobile work because they're always in immediate reach of the user. Apps on TV, however, stagnate because the incentive to go to the place where the TV is located reduces because of the additional effort of walking to that place, especially because the user has all such apps in his/her pocket. This suggests that *copying ideas is not a simple thing but actually requires careful thinking and analysis.*

Remember: innovate only on one thing that differentiates your business; copy everything else.

PART 5

YOU ARE NOT ALONE

PLAY NON-ZERO-SUM GAMES

No business delivers value to the end customer all by itself. In reality, a business does very few things within its boundaries. Everything else must come from other businesses: from renting servers on AWS to leasing offices, and from advertising on Google to buying laptops from Dell. Most of the time, such dependencies emerge naturally and evolve without any conscious effort. However, sometimes, business dependencies can (and should) be deepened explicitly through partnerships.

To grow your business, first help grow a partner's business

If nurtured well, business partnerships create positive feedback loops that help rapidly grow a business. Consider the case of Apple, a famously vertically integrated company that makes its own OS, processor, and many other phone components that other companies typically purchase from vendors. However, their iPhone App Store is proof that even Apple realizes that it can't thrive without partners. Apple supports many thousands of third-party software developers who create millions of amazing apps for the iPhone. These apps wouldn't have been possible without the underlying technology supplied by iPhone. Similarly, the iPhone wouldn't have been as successful as it is if it didn't provide the multitude of functionality that its users have now come to expect because of all the third-party apps available on the platform. So, the iPhone helped the developer community build a business on top of it, and with that, iPhone benefitted massively.

A common mistake that entrepreneurs make is to focus exclusively on end customers while neglecting to build long-term, genuine partnerships with other businesses. While customers are obviously important, partners play a vital role in opening new markets, expanding the value delivered to customers and preventing customers from switching to a competitor.

To make good partners who can help grow your business, start by understanding the motivations and drives of potential partners. Do they want money from you? Do they want access to your customers? Or do they want a promotion or marketing help? Maybe they want guidance and training in a newly emerging field? After understanding their motivations, support their business as if it was yours. Once partners become enabled around your business and you give them what they want (training, exposure, commissions), they will work hard to grow their business, which in turn will grow your business.

> **Remember:** play the long game by treating your partners' business as if it was your own and they will do the same.

BE IRREPLACEABLE IN THE VALUE CHAIN

End customers typically get the final product through a series of businesses adding value one after another. For example, consider the value chain required to bring a laptop into your hands. The production begins with suppliers of metals and raw materials which are used by manufacturers to build components like CPU, screens, and disk drives. These are then assembled to build a laptop. The

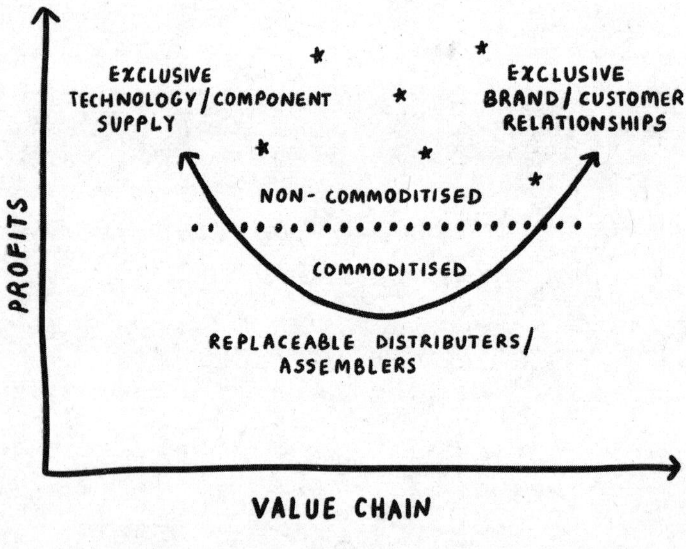

Profits typically aggregate to whoever can commoditize the other

laptop also needs software that's typically written by some other supplier like Microsoft. And, finally, the fully functional, ready-to-use laptop is shipped by a logistics company like FedEx to a warehouse. Customers transact with an online or offline seller of laptops which is typically yet another company (Amazon or BestBuy).

The entire value chain of a laptop comprises different businesses at different stages who all compete for a share of the $1,000 price of the laptop.

The key question is who gets what share of this $1,000?

The question is important because all businesses in the value chain want to maximize their share of this money but only a few are able to do so. To maximize their share of the money, all businesses try to squeeze their upstream suppliers in terms of cost and squeeze their downstream customers in terms of price. Gradually, a few players in the value chain emerge as the ones who're in the commanding position to set prices for others and everyone else has to adjust their profit margins to accommodate their demands.

How do you think Apple boasts more than a 50 per cent margin on their phones while LG exited the mobile phone business altogether citing profitability concerns?

Often, businesses that have either exclusive intellectual property or exclusive customer relationships end up commoditizing other businesses in the value chain. As a thumb rule, if a business is irreplaceable, it will eat profits of another upstream or downstream business that's undifferentiated. In fact, what suggests differentiation is not an entrepreneur's opinion but a healthy profit margin on the balance sheet.

For example, in the laptop industry, companies like Intel, ARM and Nvidia supply processors and graphics chips that are built on top of their patented intellectual property. There aren't many alternatives to microprocessor companies but there are many suppliers of metals that go into building these chips and many assemblers who use these chips to assemble computers (Lenovo, Acer, Compaq, Dell). Similarly, because laptop users are familiar with Microsoft Windows and many of their apps only run on Windows, Microsoft is in a position to dictate their own price, which computer assemblers have to pay out of the money they get from the customer. Hence, in this simplified example of the laptop industry, profits accumulate at companies that are irreplaceable. The rest of the businesses in the value chain end up struggling to make profits because competition between them drives down the money they can keep for themselves.

Another example of this is the evolving online news industry. Before Facebook or Twitter (now X) came along, people used to visit individual publication's website (like NYTimes.com or CNN.com). These publications owned the relationship with the customers, and hence accumulated the profits while commoditizing its suppliers (the journalists on their payroll). Now with Facebook and X becoming the primary mode of discovering and consuming news for many people, these publications are getting commoditized.

The surprising thing is that because of this commodification of publications, journalists who have a knack for writing content that catches attention on Facebook or X are getting de-commoditized (Substack, I'm looking at you!). Social media has reduced publications to assemblers and elevated good journalists as exclusive suppliers. Some publications tried rebelling against this process by removing themselves from Facebook, but they quickly came back as they realized that Facebook now owns customer relationships as customers weren't abandoning it anytime soon.

While genuine, non-competitive partnerships exist and you must try creating them, most businesses try to continuously squeeze other businesses wherever they can. So, you must always try to be unique and irreplaceable, while exploring alternatives for its downstream and upstream businesses to reduce dependence on them.

> **Remember:** profits accumulate to the one who's irreplaceable.

PART 6

BUILDING A DEFENSIBLE BUSINESS

SWITCHING COSTS DETERMINE THE VALUATION OF YOUR BUSINESS

The valuation of a company can seem to be shrouded in mystery. How is it possible that a startup with no products can sometimes get valued so highly that everyone is left scratching their heads, wondering if the investors have lost it?

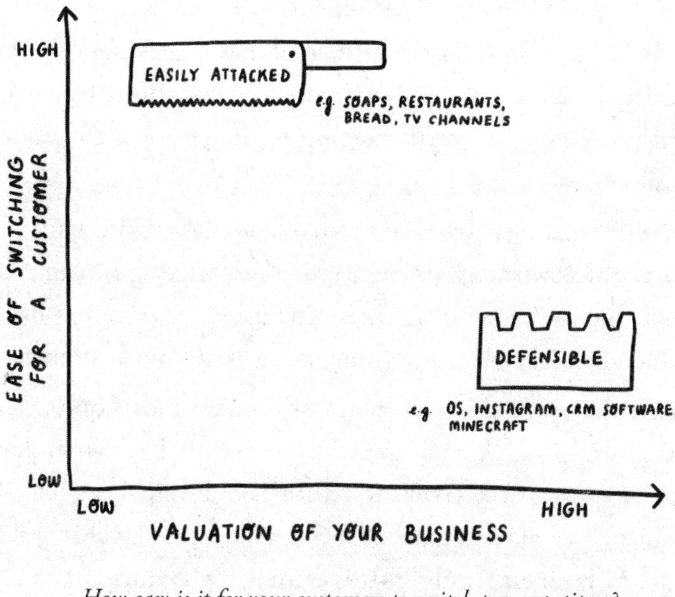

How easy is it for your customers to switch to competitors?

Like a painting at an auction, sometimes a bidding war between investors for a stake can push the valuation sky high. But such situations are rare because investors have a fiduciary duty to their limited partners to produce a return. What often happens is that basic economics drives the valuation of a business. For evolved companies, valuation is equal to how much future profits it is expected to generate for its shareholders. So, if your company is expected to generate $100 in all future profits (adjusted for interest rates/cost of capital), investors should pay $100 for acquiring its shares—why else would anyone pay more?

In a nutshell, investors value your business equal to its expected future profits. So, if your customers are able to switch easily to a competitor, potential investors see that as a risk, and hence will not value your business highly as your potential future earnings are at risk of being taken away by a competitor.

If building a business is hard, building a defensible business is harder, and that's why they're rare. Warren Buffett is one of the richest people on earth because he understood the value of defensibility early.

In old times, castles were protected by trenches filled with water which were known as moats. Such moats protected against an enemy attack as they were not easy to cross. In business, moats are whatever deters a potential competitor from taking away your customers.

Buffett explains the importance of business moats quite clearly in his 2007 letter: 'A truly great business must have an enduring "moat" that protects excellent returns on invested capital. The dynamics of capitalism guarantee that competitors will repeatedly assault any business "castle" that is earning high returns.'[1]

Moats could be patents, trade secrets or exclusive partnerships that give you access to something unique that your competitors don't have.

Perhaps the most important moat is the switching costs that your customers incur when they move from your offerings to your competitors'. If it's trivial for a customer to switch, you do not have a defensible business. To increase switching costs, get your customer to invest in your offerings. Such investment could be of various types:

- *Historical data storage*: Customers won't switch to competitors if they've stored their historical data that cannot be exported easily. Typical examples: email service providers, CRM, Facebook.
- *Habits and familiarity*: With products that are used at a high frequency (such as personal phones or browsers or soft drinks), the development of habits pose a big deterrent because to switch to something new, people will have to build new habits and relearn what's now familiar to them.
- *Sunk cost*: If customers have already paid for long-term use of a product, they're unlikely to switch to a competitor midway and waste their investment. This is why SaaS companies prefer charging annually. A classic example of this is the Gillette razor, which only works with Gillette blades.
- *Personalized value*: An offering that's unique to each customer also has a high switching cost because it's unlikely that the customer will get the same unique customization from a competitor as well. A typical example of this is operating

systems, such as Windows, Linux and Mac, which allow a user to assemble programs or apps that are uniquely suited to his/her needs. It's unlikely that the user will get the exact combination of programs in another OS. Even if there are a couple of programs that are only available on Windows that a customer uses, s/he is unlikely to switch to a Mac. Another example is Instagram, where you get to see photos from all your friends, and another app won't have your friends over (even if the app functionality is better).

All highest valuation businesses have several of these switching costs built into their products. The best example of such combined switching costs is Apple's iPhone. The unique combination of apps on its app store, storage of data and photos on iCloud and the muscle memory of its design ensure that iPhone users continue on the iPhone. And this defensibility of the iPhone's business is why markets value Apple so highly.

> **Remember**: successful businesses attract competitors. Build moats from day one of your business to protect against their attacks.

COMPETE ON COST OR QUALITY—YOU CAN'T DO BOTH

Proven physical theories are called laws because they dictate how our world operates. If there were such a 'law' of capitalism, it would probably be this: profits attract competitors who try to eliminate it by offering customers either a lower price or a higher quality.

This law thus allows for only two types of businesses to exist: cost-focused or quality-focused. Think of a McDonald's versus your neighborhood gourmet burger restaurant. Any business that tries to be both doesn't work out in the long run.

Cost-focused businesses are those that compete to give a lower-priced, standard-quality product. Since they offer products at low prices, their profit margins are typically razor thin but they make up for it by selling at high volumes. Thin margins imply that cost-focused businesses work relentlessly to keep lowering their expenses via operational efficiency and pass the majority of cost savings back to customers in the form of low prices. A new competitor typically isn't able to offer similar products at a lower price because they're not able to match the enormous operational efficiency that's required to do so.

The best example of cost-focused business is Walmart, whose 'everyday low prices' promise is made possible only because they've invested decades of effort to squeeze efficiency out of their operations, procurement, logistics, discounting and warehousing. Walmart does not promise the highest quality product or experience because they know it's impossible to do so at the price they offer products to their customers. But their customers are okay with this because they care about cheap prices more than anything else. For them, Walmart is much better than any other retailer.

Quality-focused businesses, on the other hand, compete by offering a highly differentiated product or service to their

Which game are you playing?

customers. They focus on keeping the quality of the product higher than the competitors so that it stands out in the market. Trying to differentiate the product from competitors requires paying highly for premium talent or ingredients, and because competitors are always trying to catch up, it also requires a never-ending flow of investment into R&D. That's why quality-focused businesses can't afford to offer a low price. They resist competitors by building highly differentiated products which are expensive or difficult to copy.

An example of such a business would be Apple. They have historically focused on design and innovation to stand apart from other computer and phone manufacturers. Their products are expensive because their philosophy is to aim for high quality at all costs.

In contrast to Apple, Amazon is a cost-focused business working on razor-thin profit margins. Bezos famously said 'Your margin is my opportunity.'

This shows that he believes Amazon is focused on winning customers by delivering the lowest possible price to them. However, their cloud offering, Amazon Web Services, is focused on building a highly differentiated cloud-computing platform, and therefore, it enjoys a double-digit profit margin.

Good business strategy is a combination of what you decide to do *and* what you decide not to do. In fact, deciding what not to do is perhaps more important than deciding what to do because it creates clear boundaries around your business model.

So, decide if you want to be cost-focused or quality-focused. If you lack this clarity, it's easy to fall into wishful thinking and start believing that your business can do whatever it wants. I know it sounds cool to say quality first, but smart entrepreneurs know that there's no shame in being relentlessly cost focused while offering good-enough quality. A lot of money can be made from offering lower prices and aiming for volume. (Walmart is a perfect example of this.)

> **Remember:** you can either be cost-focused or quality-focused. Don't try to be both. It doesn't work.

DO WHAT'S HARD (BECAUSE EVERYONE'S DOING WHAT'S EASY)

Business opportunities that seem easy, or those that require minimal investment, are easy for everyone (and not just you). Most people naturally gravitate towards work that's easy, enjoyable or sexy.

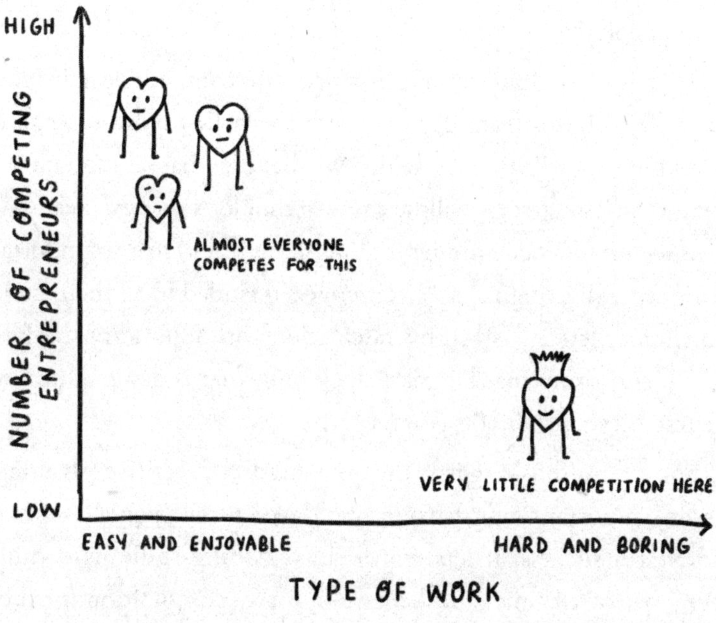

Appeal and competition is inversely related

However, the real advantage lies in doing what others aren't willing to do. Such work is either really hard, or takes an enormous amount of time or requires enormous capital, or is extremely boring and unsexy. The fewer the number of potential competitors in these less-popular domains often translates into a much higher chance of building a successful business.

A fantastic example of this is Amazon. They've focused on long-term investments into logistics, warehouses and data centres that take decades to start producing returns. This long horizon requires patience, and not all entrepreneurs or investors have it. But Jeff Bezos considers this lack of patience in other companies precisely his unfair competitive advantage.

In an interview, Bezos once said: 'If everything you do needs to work on a three-year time horizon, then you're competing against a lot of people.'

This idea of long-term thinking as a competitive advantage was clear to Bezos from day one. In his very first letter to Amazon shareholders in 1997, he said: 'We believe that a fundamental measure of our success will be the shareholder value we create over the long term.' The reminder for long-term thinking is so important to him that this original 1997 letter gets included in all their annual shareholder letters. Given his fascination with long-term thinking, it's not surprising that he got a clock built that is designed to keep accurate time for 10,000 years.

Long-term thinking isn't the only 'hard' competitive advantage. It's an important one in our world where everyone is chasing short-term success. It lets you focus on doing really hard things over a period of time, and hence eliminates competition for those projects. Other competitive advantages could be doing what's unsexy or boring (like waste management, tax and accounting, or mainframes).

A word of caution: it's easy to convince yourself that you're long-term oriented or doing something that is hard while your actions gravitate towards short-term or easier stuff.

> **Remember:** competitive advantage doesn't come by doing what's easy. It comes by things that others aren't willing or able to do.

NEVER STOP CREATING NETWORK EFFECTS IN YOUR BUSINESS

A business is said to have network effects if each new customer increases the value for all other customers. Take a telephone network. Each new customer with a telephone line helps increase the value of the network for all other customers because now more people can talk to each other than before.

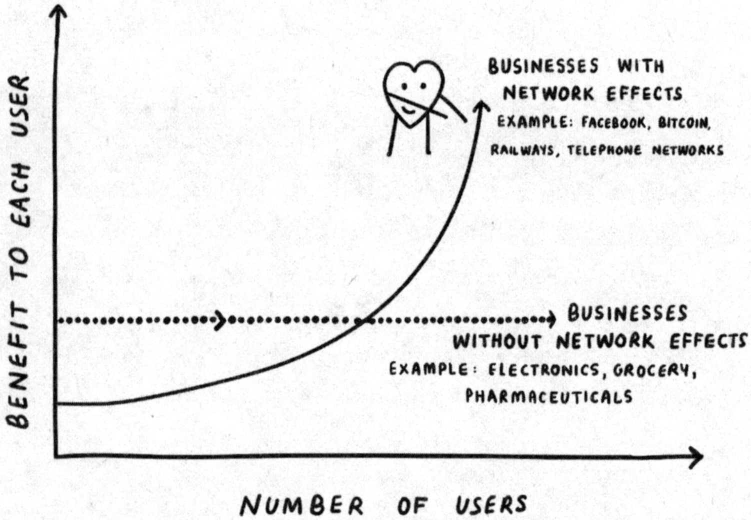

Network effects, once triggered, become unstoppable

Contrast this to other businesses such as the appliances manufacturing business. It's obvious to see that if I sell a toaster to someone, none of my other customers benefit from that sale.

A business with strong network effect gains a strong competitive advantage over time. A customer choosing between two alternatives will logically go with the one that delivers more value, which is often the one with stronger network effects. Since businesses with network effects keep attracting new customers who make such network effects stronger, these businesses soon become almost impossible to beat in their category. Network effects are like escape velocity—once over a threshold, such businesses become practically unbeatable. Think Facebook, WhatsApp and Instagram. The value of these apps is not in the technology they provide but in the network of people using them.

Network effects can go beyond this telephone or WhatsApp kind of networks where people talk to each other. The more general idea of network effects is positive feedback loops that make a business stronger over time. These loops are simple logical ideas that connect various aspects of a business model in a way that makes business growth self-reinforcing.

Amazon started with one such positive feedback loop (also known as a flywheel):

Network effects are often hidden or unintuitive but every successful business has them. For example, Google has no obvious positive feedback loop or network effect. However, for Google, the data generated by their users is a kind of network effect. The more data they have on searching patterns, the better their algorithms get, which improves results for all users.

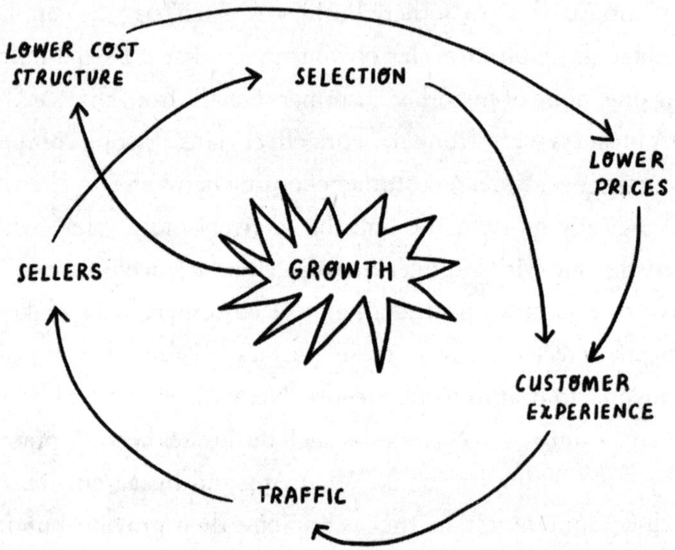

Amazon's flywheel

Similarly, a business like Netflix has a positive feedback loop because the more customers there are on their app, the more movies they can buy or produce, which then benefits all their customers.

> **Remember:** positive feedback loops gradually build unbreachable moats for a business. So you must strive to find not just one positive feedback loop in your business, but as many as you possibly can.

PART 7

ACQUIRING CUSTOMERS

ALL NEW PRODUCTS COMPETE WITH CUTE CAT MEMES FOR ATTENTION

You get pitched by other companies all the time. Yesterday, you might have seen thousands of ads. How many of those can you recall? If you're like most people, it'll be difficult for you to recall even a single message. At best, if you stress hard, you'd be able to recall only a few things.

If you, the entrepreneur, cannot recall ads or marketing messages that you are exposed to, how do you expect your customers to remember your pitches?

Nobody loves marketing messages

Entrepreneurs spend a significant amount of time creating their campaigns, so they become biased into assuming that if their target customer sees the ad, she will remember it and take action whenever the need for the marketed product arises. But that's not how customers' minds work. What happens instead is this: people see an ad and immediately move on with their life as if nothing happened.

That's because all marketing messages compete for attention with things that people want to spend their attention on. If people want to focus on their work, a sales call is a distraction. If people want to spend time browsing Instagram, a TV ad in the background is a distraction. If people want to read articles in the newspaper, a banner ad is a distraction. That's why they'll not pick up phone calls from unknown numbers, switch off the TV or simply install ad blockers.

Due to this blindness to marketing messages, you need to take a more nuanced approach. While designing your campaigns, focus on these three aspects:

- *Motivation of the customer*: In your marketing communications, address upfront why a prospective customer should pay attention. That 'why' is never about the product, it's always about the person and her desires. Nobody wants to buy products. Instead, they want to satisfy one of their unmet desires (and the product is simply a means to that end). If a customer who receives a marketing message doesn't relate to the 'why' of the ad or cannot easily find or understand such 'why', the ad becomes a distraction. So you should not just articulate a clear reason for the prospective customer to pay attention, but also avoid spending money on targeting people who don't have that desire hoping that an ad will create such desire in them. Desire-creation doesn't happen that easily because an ad in itself doesn't do anything. People forget the ads they see.

- *Emotion evoked*: People remember things that resonate with them emotionally. Marketing messages should hit the prospective customer on some emotional level—they should laugh, get surprised or feel special. Unless they feel something, they will quickly forget that they ever saw or heard about something from your company.
- *Repetition*: One-shot marketing is worse than no marketing because it costs money without giving results. People forget things all the time. The only way to ensure that people remember that your product or service exists when they need it is to continuously refresh their memory about it. Yes, it's expensive but that's the only way it works. You should rather reduce the number of people you reach but ensure that you reach them again and again via multiple channels. It's not the width of reach that matters; it's the depth.

To remember these three elements of marketing, you can use the shorthand MER, which stands for motivation, emotion and repetition.

Remember: most people consider marketing an intrusion into their lives. So, marketing isn't about developing a message and reaching out to the target market. Instead, it is all about crafting relevant, engaging messages that actually benefit and delight prospective customers—and doing that repeatedly.

PEOPLE DECIDE THROUGH THEIR GUT AND JUSTIFY THROUGH THEIR BRAIN

Even though the capacity to reason is a highlight for our species, most of our decisions are made emotionally. Who we fall in love with isn't rational but we can always find good reasons to justify our choice of partner.

Similarly, our reasons for choosing to use certain products or services often have a strong emotional factor, even though when asked, we will happily give rational justifications for the same.

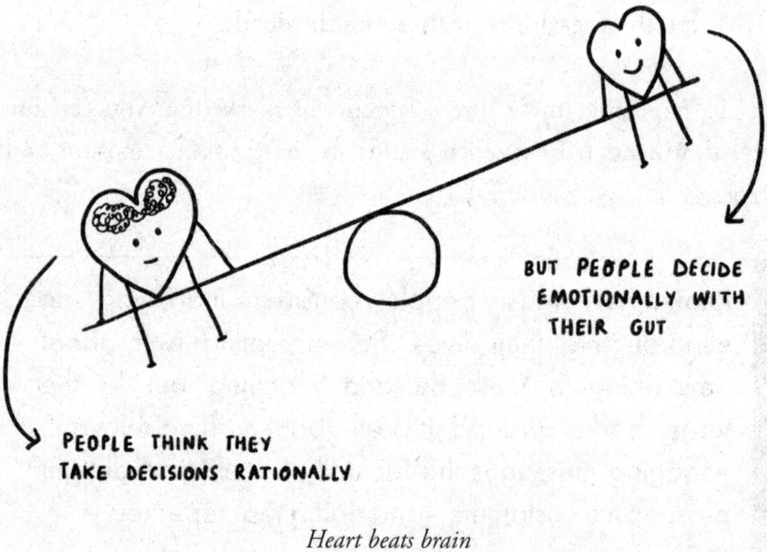

Heart beats brain

One of the biggest mistakes an entrepreneur can make is to assume that potential customers will judge their product from a cost/benefit point of view. When a product is pitched to them, customers don't spend time evaluating its features and then decide if they're going to buy it or not. Rather, their first reaction is from the gut. The pitch (in form of advertisement, website or a sales call) has to cross many evolved defenses before customers even start paying attention to what's on offer.

You are a stranger to a customer, and we're evolved to be skeptical of strangers. Imagine that in a primitive hunter–gatherer society, many hundreds of thousands of years ago, someone comes along and suggests that there's a bounty of food behind that hill. You'd expect people in that group to be skeptical of the claim because one, why would a stranger tell others about benefits that he himself can make use of, and two, what if there's hidden danger or cost which benefits the stranger and that's why he's enticing us?

So, people evolved to be skeptical at first of claims from strangers. A pitch from a new company is nothing but a pitch for a bounty from a stranger.

People's gut reaction to a pitch is likely made up of hundreds of little heuristics that evolved over thousands of years to assist human decision-making. But we can isolate a few key factors that can help people decide in favour of a stranger's pitch:

- *Trust*: Are you giving a reason for people to trust? Research shows that people form a gut-level opinion on others as soon as they meet them. This initial impression tells them how skeptical and careful they should be in their interaction with a stranger. For example, a sales person who dresses nicely or a website that looks premium increases trust because people naturally assume that the stranger has enough resources himself so the likelihood of him cheating others for more resources is low. This property of good looks equals more trust is exploited by many in the business world because it works.

- *Social proof*: Do you have anyone else to back you up? A stranger who comes with a proof of someone familiar backing his claims is much more likely to be believed than the one who just says: 'Trust me, I'm telling the truth'. This is why B2B websites and pitches are filled with social proof of prominent companies using their services, and this is also the same reason celebrities are effective in marketing. However, the most effective social proof is from a peer, which is why word of mouth is the most effective form of marketing (though it's terribly hard to influence—your product or service has to be good enough that people talk about it by themselves without any prodding from your side).
- *Evidence*: What evidence do you have to back your claim? It's just not enough to be likable and come with social proof. A successful pitch consists of evidence to back claims. However, it's important to note that people only invest their time in listening to and evaluating evidence if first they feel they can trust you and you have enough social proof for them to even begin paying attention to what you're saying. The order of these factors matter. You cannot overwhelm people with evidence first and then give reasons to trust. They will simply tune out and you'll lose them.
- *Effort:* For the benefits you're promising, what are you asking in return (money, time, reputation)? If you're asking for

too much, people can still reject your pitch even if you're trustworthy, have social proof backing you up, and provide sufficient evidence for your claims. The golden rule of marketing is that people have to believe that they'll be getting much more than what they're required to spend. Benefits don't just have to be marginally better than costs; they have to be substantially better.

> **Remember:** to get the sale, first dismantle people's automatic skepticism of strangers; only then should s/he proceed with the pitch.

ALWAYS DELIVER MORE THAN YOU ASK

Sellers always know more about the products they're selling than the buyers. While evaluating a potential purchase, buyers often feel they don't have enough information to know whether what they're getting is worth the cost (in time, money, effort). Even when the seller gives information about the value the buyer will get, buyers suspect because both honest and dishonest sellers say similar things.

As buyers can't perfectly distinguish between good products and bad products, they typically end up wanting to pay (in time, money, effort) much less even for honestly no-brainer kinds of deals. In many markets, this drives away good, honest sellers leaving only dishonest sellers (which further aggravates the mistrust). The most famous example of this is the used cars market, but some versions of this play out in all markets.

Big, newly launched, obviously good products can fail because of the mistrust in the market for new tech products. Honest entrepreneurs get penalized in the market because of other dishonest entrepreneurs (who overpromise and underdeliver). So your first job as an entrepreneur becomes winning the trust of the market. (This is why brands and social proof matter.)

But, trust is not binary. Customers are continuously updating their beliefs about what your product can do for them. With every interaction a customer has with your brand, she is evaluating the costs (what she'll lose) against benefits (what she'll gain). Money is one of the many costs. Other costs are time, effort and reputation investment.

When it comes to costs, it is important to understand that people are loss averse. They'd much rather not lose what they have than gain something new. For example, most people will avoid taking a bet where there is a 50 per cent chance of winning $20,000 but a 50 per cent chance of losing $10,000 even though the expected reward is positive (0.5*20k – 0.5*10k). But almost everyone will probably take a bet where there is a 50 per cent chance of winning a million dollars and a 50 per cent chance of losing $1,000.

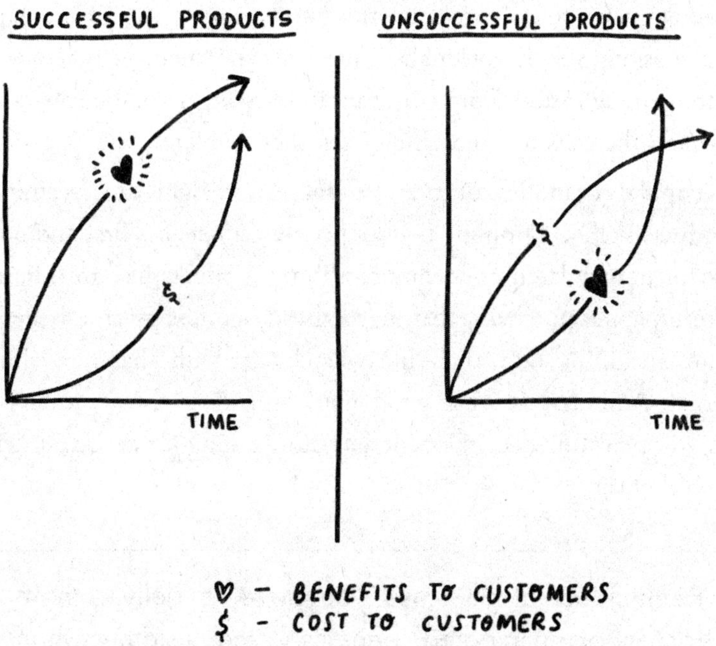

Success = At all times (benefits > cost)

This shows that in order to make a decision, people expect benefits to be substantially more than the costs. Your product has to be perceived as a guaranteed lottery to them, right from the get go.

This is because, at any point, when their estimate of costs (that they know for sure—fill a form, talk to sales, $299/month cost) seems to be higher than the evidence of current and future value, they drop off from the interactions with a brand and abandon their journey. Good salespeople understand this dynamic and start with the conversations that put people at ease, and only at the very end, ask something tangible from them (like a request for another meeting or a trial implementation).

Your interactions with customers should be a dialogue (and not a monologue) where you're delivering more value to them than what you're asking for. If you make a big ask from them before they've gotten enough value from you, they'll drop off. If you deliver value first and then ask for something later, they'll oblige.

Popular examples of brands that do it right are freemium products such as Dropbox that let people get benefits first and only ask for money later. For many consumer products like an iPhone, before people purchase, they have already gotten psychic benefits from imagining how their life will change with that new shiny phone. And that is what good marketing does for a product—convince customers of the benefits before asking for an investment from them.

> **Remember:** at all times you have to deliver more (actual or anticipated) benefits to the customers than the investments you require them to make.

PART 8

MAKING MONEY

GENERATING PROFIT REQUIRES CREATIVITY

Businesses don't exist to make revenue, they exist to make profits. But the lure of revenue is hard to resist. Many big companies that generate billions of dollars attract admiration from entrepreneurs but when the news of them struggling to be viable appears, this admiration turns into shock and confusion.

How can a big company go bankrupt? You may have heard of this before, but a sure-shot way of making revenue is to offer $110 for

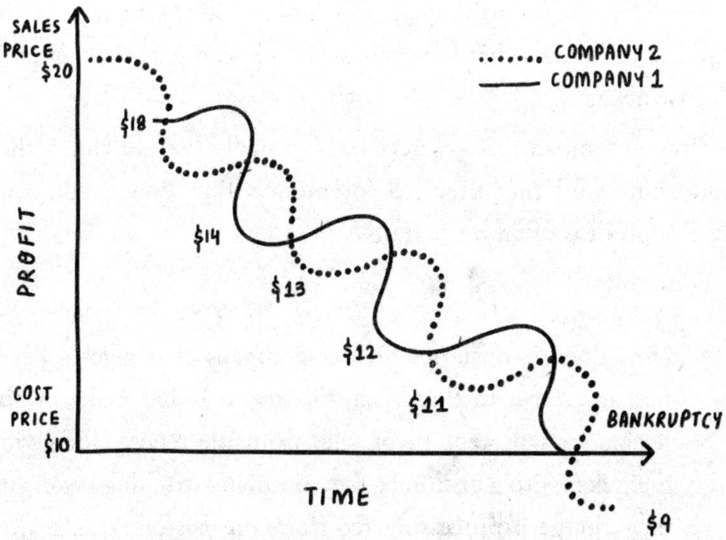

Competition eats away all profit

$100. If you open this business, you'll have no problem attracting customers and you'll not even need to do any marketing (except when a new competitor springs up, who offers $120 for $100). This example may seem worthy of nothing more than a chuckle, but this business model is actually very common. Many startups grew by essentially handing out money to customers (in the form of discounts and cashbacks).

How do you convert this revenue into profit?

Well, that's what is non-trivial. It requires creativity in a business model to keep profits from dissolving in the environment. In a head-on battle between competitors, prices are lowered until no company makes a profit. All obvious sources of profits get hunted soon by either large players or nimble startups who undercut your margins. The business equivalent of Tolstoy's famous quote 'All happy families are alike; each unhappy family is unhappy in its own way'[1] could very well be: All unprofitable companies are alike (engaged in the stupidity of head-on battle); each profitable company is profitable in its own way.

How a company makes revenue is usually very obvious: they make some stuff that they sell for money. But, how a company makes a profit is often mysterious.

For example:

- How does a consumer finance company that gives a 0 per cent interest loan (like Bajaj Finserv in India) make profit? It charges a percentage of sales from the retailer for giving them access to a customer they normally wouldn't have, and they charge a processing fee from the customer, and they have customer purchase appliances on non-discounted, retail price. (So customers lose out on a potential discount they could have had otherwise.) By combining all these methods, they make healthy profit even as they advertise a 0 per cent interest loan.

- How does truck rental company U-haul in a commodity market make a profit in spite of having cheaper rates than the competition? They make all their profit on accessories like boxes and other packaging material and none on the actual hauling services.
- Why does Costco, a big US retailer, generate profits while other retailers are struggling? Because they charge a membership fee and that's where Costco's profits come from (and not through selling stuff). They're a club, not a retailer.

The entire complexity of a business exists to generate that tiny, little profit from someplace that isn't obvious. So a cinema hall from the outside looks like it is in the entertainment business, but on closer analysis, it is in the food and hospitality business. The entertainment side of things is to get a captive, hungry group of people who you can then charge a lot of money to fund losses for their hyper-competitive movie screening business.

The next time you come across a business that has been there for quite a while, pause and think about how they make a profit. It is a fun exercise!

Also remember the famous quote by Peter Theil—'competition is for losers'—because entrepreneurs in your industry think like Bezos, who said, 'your margin is my opportunity'.

Remember: to survive as a business, you need to make a profit. To make a profit, you need to avoid competition, and to avoid competition, you need to be creative.

WHAT PEOPLE PAY FOR SOMETHING IS DETERMINED BY ITS PERCEIVED ALTERNATIVES

People don't know how much they should be paying for a particular product. Evolution has trained us to be skeptical of strangers' claims. By default, people will always feel they're getting ripped off. So, while evaluating how much to pay, they try to guess what alternatives they have and how much such alternatives cost. Hence, the positioning of a product becomes the primary criteria by which the price is judged by people.

But, often, it's also the other way around. Especially for new brands, price serves as an anchor to the customer for deciding which category to slot the product in. For example, the price of a newly launched car slots it either in the luxury or the mid-range or the budget market. It matters less if the car is actually luxury or not, but if the price of the car is similar to Mercedes or BMW, the expectations of the consumer and their willingness to pay will be similar to Mercedes or BMW.

This suggests that no single company has the leverage to charge whatever it wants to. Customer expectations for the right price for a product are guided by what alternatives are available in the market and how much those things cost. Startups have no option but to play within the market of perceived alternatives and charge similar to what those alternatives are charging. For example, the internet has made consumers habituated to free news, information, and videos. A startup that wants to charge for information has an uphill battle because, in the minds of consumers, the price of information is close to nil (even though the value they get from such information is high). So, value pricing doesn't work out—water is valuable but people don't pay a lot for it.

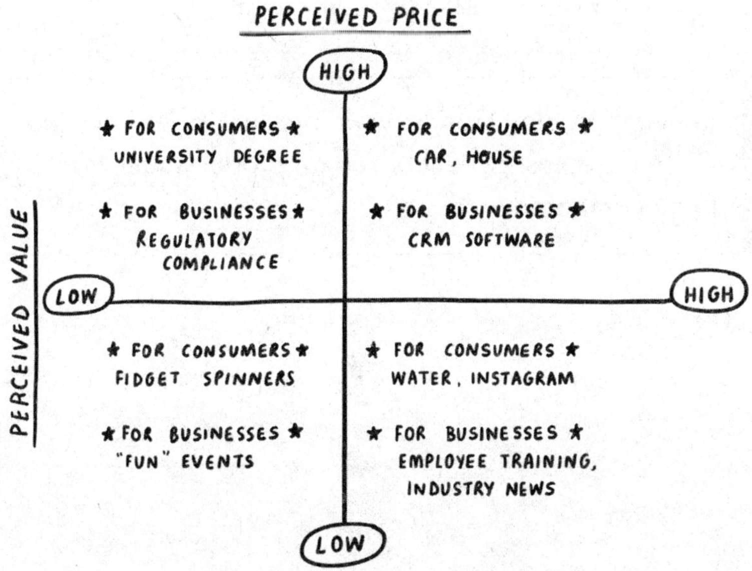

Where does your product lie on the value-price 2×2 matrix?

This is also why a lower price is not always better. When products offered are too cheap, they send a signal about quality. Especially in enterprises where they're used to purchasing software and services worth many thousands of dollars, a product that's only priced a few dollars is perceived to be meant for small businesses and not enterprises.

So, price your products not based on the value you're providing, but what your customers are used to paying for offerings closest in their minds to your offering. This also means that through right messaging and positioning, you have an opportunity to influence what your customers compare the offering to and hence what you are able to charge. For example, if you're launching an information product, don't call it a report and have customers compare it to freely available information on the internet. Position it as consulting and customers will be able to pay dearly for it.

> **Remember:** don't price your product based on the value it creates, price it based on products you want it to be compared with.

YOUR PRODUCT'S PRICE DETERMINES YOUR ENTIRE PLAYBOOK

The price of your products will end up determining all the other components of your business. This happens because price influences the number and kinds of customers in the market (higher the price, lower the number of customers).

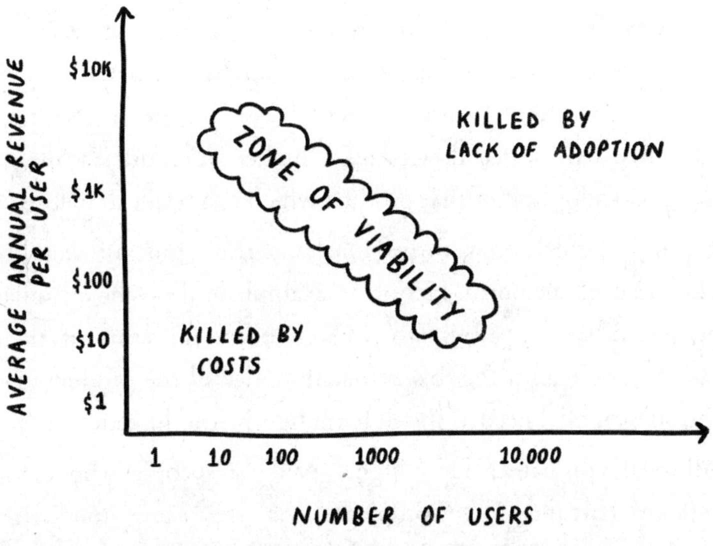

Zone of business viability

(adapted from 'Five ways to build $100 million business'[1]*)*

This in turn determines:

- the distribution channels you need to build in order to reach your customers profitably,
- the cost of customer acquisition,
- your sales and service process, and
- all that, in turn, determines your organizational structure.

In other words, setting the price of your products is akin to choosing a highly specific playbook for building your business.

The tight relationship between price and business model means that a mismatch between the two leads to failure. This failure can happen in two ways. First, if you keep the price low in a market that has a limited number of customers, you cap your revenue. The limited revenue opportunity means that your startup can get killed by costs. The other case is keeping a price higher for a market that has a very large number of customers. In such cases, competition usually drives the price down and a higher price usually means slower or no adoption of that product which can result in failure.

Business models that thrive in the narrow zone of viability quickly become the norm. Hence, an example of this is how similar enterprise B2B companies are to each other in terms of their playbook. The reason for this is that the price of the product and the business model needed to sell it are tightly interlinked.

All B2B companies have highly paid salespeople who chase the same Fortune 500 companies via the same marketing channels (events, cold calls or analysts). All such companies have account managers who are experts in relationship building and communication. The user interface takes a back seat for enterprise products as customization and adaptation to an enterprise are a higher priority.

Contrast this with how B2B companies targeting small businesses operate. Since their target market comprises tens of thousands of businesses, each of whom pays tens of dollars per month, they cannot afford to sell through a salesperson. They need to rely on platforms like Adwords or Google search for customer acquisition and their products' user interface has to be slick enough for self-service.

> **Remember:** a large business (> $100 million annual revenue) can be built for a product at any price. But as soon as either price is chosen, the market and business model gets chosen for you (and vice versa).

PART 9

PITCHING YOUR STARTUP

YOUR ELEVATOR PITCH SHOULDN'T BE ABOUT YOU

Entrepreneurs generally think of their pitch as something that needs to be about what they're doing. This interpretation is understandable because if anyone you meet ends up asking them what you do, you'd faithfully tell them what you do.

Unfortunately, a pitch that's focused on you often ends up with the listener quickly losing interest.

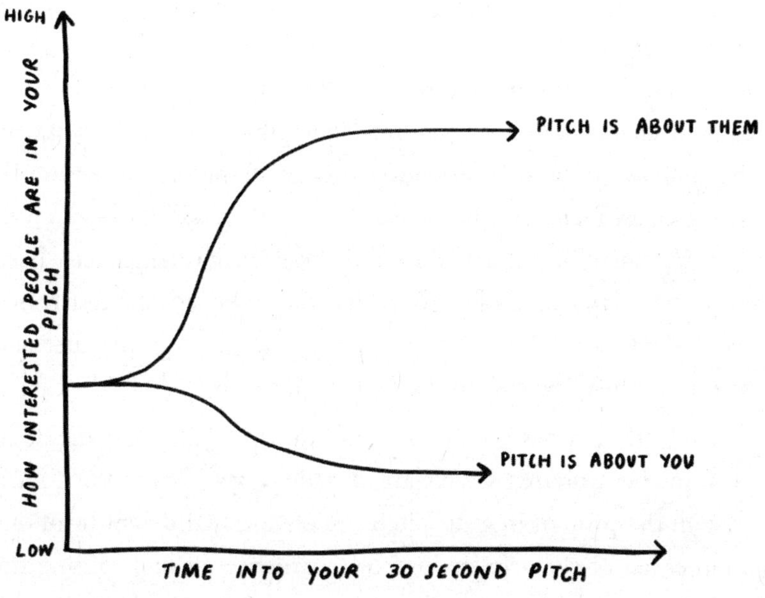

Always make the pitch about them

This is because even though people ask what you do with good intentions, they usually do not actually deeply care about what you do. What people care about is themselves, which suggests that a pitch should start and end with them and revolve around the world they live in.

In short, your pitch should start with talking about the audience's aspirations and goals and only then talk about how your startup helps fulfil those aspirations. For example, instead of talking about how many features you have in your CRM product, your pitch should be about how salespeople lose four hours a day updating customer information which comes at a loss of $50k per salesperson per year and how your product helps salespeople recover those four hours every day.

A fantastic example of such a pitch is Elon Musk Tesla's battery product Powerwall. As you watch it, notice how Elon starts his talk by highlighting why the audience should care about what he's going to say. For doing that, he points out greenhouse gas pollution and climate change—two drastic challenges that impact everyone in the audience (and their families). After grabbing their attention by telling them precisely what's wrong with the world, he goes on to show the possibility of a world where these two challenges have been solved via batteries. Only after he has the audience's interest firmly established does he start talking about their battery product and how it can help the audience transition into a better world.

Andy Raskin has a fantastic write-up on common elements of great pitches (internet-search 'greatest pitch ever andy raskin'). Even though the content in great pitches is obviously different from one another, all of them follow a similar structure of highlighting the audience's pain first, then showing a possibility of a better world, then highlighting the barriers to that better world, and at last introducing the product features as things that will help overcome such barriers.

This perspective shift from what you're doing to why the listener should care doesn't just help you in making a great pitch; it also helps you become more customer-centric (and less feature-centric). And this orientation away from you, towards the market, ultimately helps all aspects of your business.

So, here's a fun exercise you can try. For your startup, try making a version of the pitch where your product is mentioned only at the very end of it (and almost in passing). The bulk of your pitch should be about the listener and her goals.

If the listener is not your target user (e.g. it's for hiring or raising funds), you obviously can't use the same pitch. The pitch has to be customized to each listener, as per their goals. Your potential customers should hear a different pitch than your potential investors, who in turn should hear a different pitch than the people you're trying to hire.

> **Remember:** never make your pitch about yourself. It has to be about the one getting pitched and her goals.

GET PRESS BY GIVING JOURNALISTS SOMETHING SURPRISING

Journalists don't get excited about new products and features the same way an entrepreneur does.

This is because:

- First, a journalist gets hundreds of pitches every day and your launch announcement is profitably no different than the many hundreds of launch announcements sitting in her inbox.
- Second, aliens visiting Earth is news but your product's new feature is certainly not news.

News is something that caters to the innate human curiosity about the new and surprising. There is a reason why one death in a tragic car accident gets covered as news but thousands of deaths every day due to preventable diseases in poor countries don't make it into the news. The former is surprising. People want to know how that particular accident happened. The latter is a statistic, a daily occurrence that people are familiar with and after a while becomes pretty boring to read.

So, to get a journalist's attention, you have to get into the mindset of being a journalist yourself. Given the almost infinite number of things they can read online, people choose a few pieces that catch their attention (and those are usually surprising, breakthrough, or controversial). Similarly, a journalist chooses to read only the pitches that catch her attention among the hundreds of pitches that get sent daily.

Next time you try to get into the press, try answering why the journalist should pick your piece to cover instead of all other attention-grabbing events happening in the world.

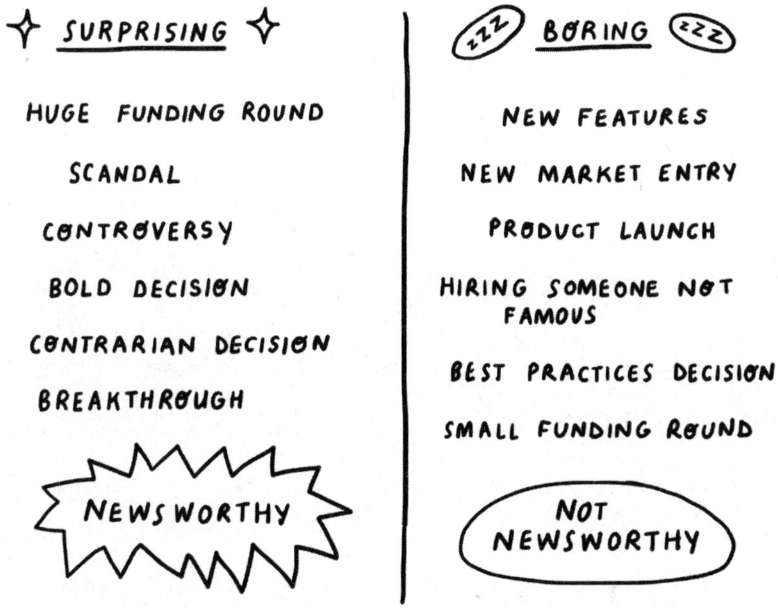

Know what's newsworthy

Don't talk about the boring. Highlight only the surprising part of your announcement. If there's none, don't spend effort and money on doing press releases.

> **Remember:** to be in the news, understand what usually is news.

RAISE FUNDING BY SHOWING HOW YOU CAN RAISE EVEN MORE FUNDING

Fundraising is an exercise in demonstrating how your company can generate financial returns for the investor.

Different types of investors have different risk–reward expectations why they end up specializing. For example, a bank as

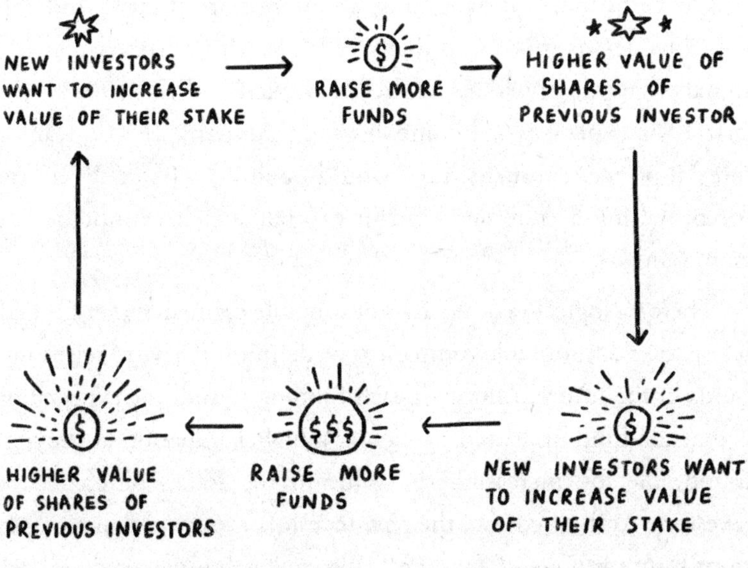

Investors are interested in their returns. Tell them how you'll help them get it.

an institution is risk-averse. They're okay with a relatively smaller return but they want to make sure that such return is guaranteed.

On the other hand, funds specializing in seed-stage funding know that most of their investments will fail, and hence to cover for those duds, they expect to fund only the opportunities with the potential to generate 100x returns. The few 100x returning opportunities and most of the others not returning anything means that on average they end up generating a decent financial return on their entire fund.

Not understanding the motivation of an investor class is a sure-shot way of an unsuccessful fundraise. Pitching to a bank that you're building a great product is likely a waste of time. They want their guaranteed 10 per cent return, and it's immaterial whether you generate that return via a great product or by selling bread.

On the other hand, talking about how profitable and safe your business is to a VC is likely to be a waste of time because it signals that your business is already peaked and the 100x return that a VC expects won't come via your company. If VCs wanted safe 10 per cent returns, they would open up a bank. VCs exist for providing a different kind of capital, which cannot be had from banks.

There's a logical reason why unprofitable companies get funded. It's because unprofitable companies, by definition, have to raise more funds in the future. And with each funding round, the expectation is that the funding would happen at a higher valuation at the next round, thereby increasing the value of the stakes purchased by investors. And, of course, the new investors expect to make money from future rounds of funding. This is why companies don't raise funds for safety or survival and keep them in their banks. VCs expect the raised funds to be spent within 12–18 months so that another round is raised soon, and with it, the value of their shares goes up. The end game of VC-led funding rounds is a company IPOing and eventually letting retail investors buy shares from initial investors at a premium.

All this means that to raise funds from VCs, the company has to show a path to becoming big enough to IPO. For VCs, a great product, a good team and good business fundamentals are important but secondary considerations. The primary concern is whether a particular business can keep on raising funds until it goes public or becomes important enough to be acquired.

Remember: understand what drives VCs and then decide whether you're ready to commit your company to that path. If the answer is yes, the entire focus of the funding pitch must be on opportunity size and growth potential because that's what matters to VCs.

RECRUIT EXCEPTIONAL PEOPLE BY SHOWING THEM A PROMISED LAND

At its core, a recruitment strategy is indistinguishable from a marketing strategy. Entrepreneurs end up spending a lot of time understanding the market, talking to customers building personas, and customizing their marketing messages to customer segments. However, they often fail to realize that recruiting people to work for you is no different from recruiting customers to use your product.

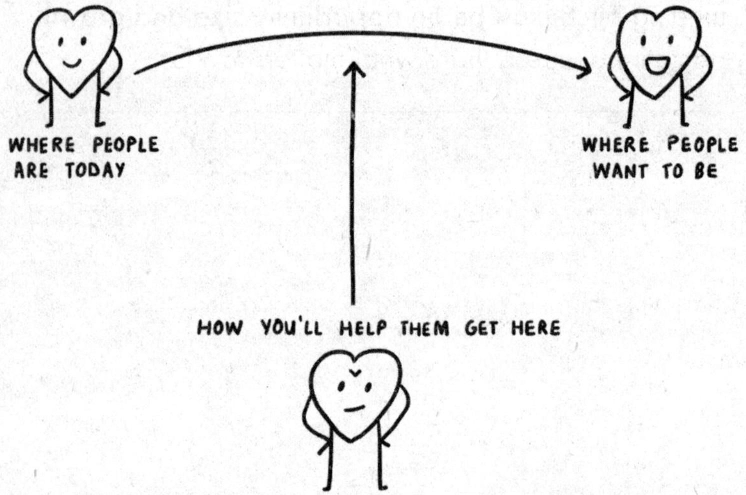

To recruit exceptional people, you have to first understand what drives them

Of course, it's true that you're asking for money from customers while you're offering to pay money to prospective employees. However, for exceptional people, the money offered is a commodity because many other companies are offering them the same or an even higher amount of money. Exceptional people never look for jobs; jobs look for them.

If you feel people will work for you because of the salary you're offering, you'll end up attracting only those kinds of people who want a safe, stress-free job that pays a regular salary. There's nothing wrong with it but then that should be your explicit decision.

People who can add higher-than-average value to your company require a higher-than-average treatment during recruitment. In all likelihood, they're not looking for just another gig. To attract such people, you need to understand what's frustrating them in their current job and what they want out of an ideal career. Is it a lot more money? Is it less interference from the manager? Is it coaching? Is it working on a new challenge?

Just like different customer segments have different needs, different talent segments have different drives. Your recruitment pitch has to be customized to those drives. If you keep harping on about how great your product is while the star employee that you're chasing is looking for freedom from micromanagement, your message is going to fall flat. Similarly, if you keep talking about how much freedom your culture allows to employees while that particular employee wants to make a million dollars through stock options, you're not going to be successful in hiring that person.

> **Remember:** treat your recruitment like marketing and prospective talent like prospective customers.

PART 10

HOW INVESTORS THINK

YOUR BUSINESS IS WORTH ALL FUTURE PROFITS IT IS EXPECTED TO GENERATE

It's easy to get bewildered by the billion-dollar valuations of loss-making startups. If you've ever wondered why anyone would pay for a company that's not making any money, you're not alone.

Early in a company's life when there is much uncertainty about its future, the valuation process is more of an art than a science.

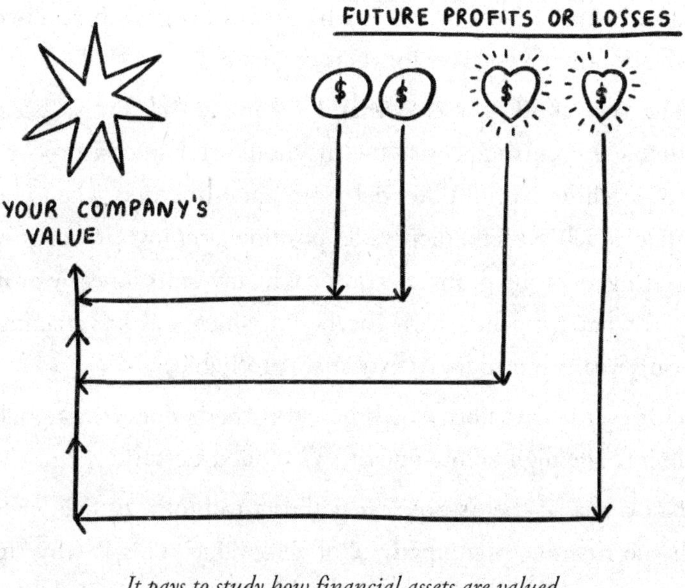

It pays to study how financial assets are valued

But, even as an art, startup valuation is grounded on a very simple financial principle that an asset is worth discounted profits it is expected to produce over its lifetime. The term discounted means that the cash in the near term is more valuable than the cash in the long term. On the internet, it's easy to find the exact formula for calculating the discounted cashflow.

However, more important than the formula is its implications.

The first implication is that investors expect rapid revenue growth, followed by a focus on profitability. A startup typically requires upfront investment before the product hits the market. This suggests that investors actually expect losses in the initial years. With these losses that are in the near term, because of the future discounting factor, the only way investors can justify a positive valuation of the company today is if future profits are substantially larger than the losses incurred today. This expectation of future astronomical profits is what drives the growth-at-all-costs expectation that VCs have for their companies.

The typical VC thesis is that a company can always become profitable by cutting costs, but it shouldn't cut costs too soon before reaching its full potential. Sometimes it works when young companies achieve a market-leader position after loss-driven growth and start generating profits to compensate investors for early profits. This is what happened with Facebook, which was loss-making in the early years, but today, is extremely profitable.

However, the majority of times, this thesis doesn't materialize, leading to the high failure rate of VC-funded startups.

Know that if there's no clear pathway to profit, no matter how high the revenue, a company is of zero value. This is why smart entrepreneurs have their eyes on both aspects: loss-fuelled growth of the company and its transition into a profit-making machine. Just revenue is worth nothing if all of it goes into expenses and shareholders, and investors get nothing in return.

The second implication of discounted cash flow is that founders of many profitable businesses don't realize the value of their businesses. They feel pressured by the billion-dollar valuations given by VCs to other businesses. It's important to realize that the billion-dollar valuation of a loss-making company is entirely dependent on future prospects and, with a high failure rate, could get down to zero. On the other hand, a profit-making business has much more substance to justify a non-zero valuation.

> **Remember:** the endgame of all businesses is a stream of profits for shareholders. Growth for growth's sake doesn't mean anything. Only growth in future streams of profit matters, and until that becomes a reality, it's just an expectation in someone's head.

RETURN-ON-INVESTED-CAPITAL IS ALL YOU NEED

The financial purpose of a business is to generate over its lifetime a higher return for shareholders than what they would have gotten by investing in risk-free options (such as government bonds).

Imagine an entrepreneur with a business proposal, and she requires $100 as the initial investment. She reaches out to you and pitches her idea to seek your investment. To make a decision, you'll probably analyse and estimate how much return you'd get in return for the money you give her. If you usually get 6 per cent interest annually in a savings bank account (which happens in India), you would expect a higher return than that from the entrepreneur (especially since there's a risk of losing your entire $100 while your money in the bank is virtually risk-free).

$$\text{RETURN ON INVESTED CAPITAL} = \frac{\text{TOTAL PROFITS (AFTER TAX) GENERATED FROM AN INVESTMENT OVER LIFETIME}}{\text{TOTAL INVESTMENT}}$$

ROIC: one metric to rule them all

The entrepreneur succeeds if she's able to deliver you a much higher return than you would have gotten from relatively 'risk-free' investments such as government bonds.

Since ROIC is how investors track the performance of their investment, it automatically becomes the most important metric through which entrepreneurs and companies are judged. Higher ROIC directly translates into more attractiveness of a business and hence, garners higher multiples for valuation.

Warren Buffett is one of the most successful investors of all time, and this is what he said in his 1992 Berkshire Hathaway Shareholder Letter: 'The best business to own is one that over an extended period can employ large amounts of incremental capital at very high rates of return.'

ROIC is not just important for investors but is also a fantastic decision criterion for entrepreneurs when they're deciding which area or project to invest in. It's a no-brainer to invest in projects where lifetime returns from the investment are expected to be much higher than what you'd get in 'risk-free' investments (also called cost of capital).

ROIC also explains why companies that give out dividends to their shareholders are generally valued less than companies that retain the earnings or don't generate earnings at all. In the former case, shareholders deduce that the company has run out of investment opportunities that could provide a return higher than risk-free return. And if a business can't compound money at a faster rate than a bank, investors would rather put their money elsewhere.

An important caveat in calculating ROIC is lifetime returns (discounted by an appropriate discount factor) and not just immediate returns. That is what drives many tech companies to invest aggressively in user acquisition because they know that the lifetime revenue from acquired users that stick with the product over the years will justify high upfront acquisition costs.

> **Remember:** a business is valued highly if it's expected to regularly generate returns much higher than the 'risk-free' returns that investors get in a savings bank account.

GREAT ENTREPRENEURS THINK LIKE INVESTORS

There are many stakeholders of a business. There are employees, customers, suppliers, management, directors, shareholders, investors, investors' investors, the government and society at large. Things are fine when everyone's interests are perfectly aligned.

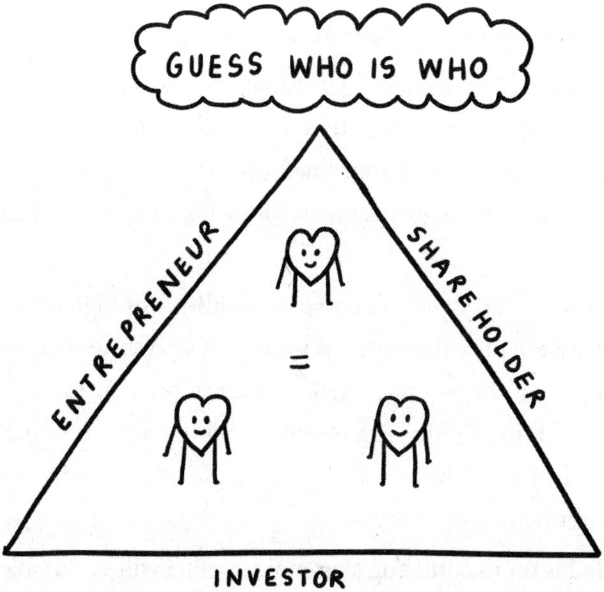

You'd not be able to guess because there is no difference

But as the number of stakeholders increases, it becomes harder to keep everyone happy. When this happens, an entrepreneur must choose whose interest must be prioritized. The choice, in practice, is hard, because some stakeholders are definitely going to be unhappy when decisions don't go their way. (Say, when an entrepreneur lays off employees.)

In theory, though, decision-making is simple. Shareholders and investors will only remain invested in the business if they see (risk-adjusted) returns on their capital higher than what they could get elsewhere (say with government bonds or public equity markets). And a business wouldn't exist if shareholders lose faith and start selling their stake at whatever price they can get. So, because a business wouldn't exist without people who fund it, its main goal boils down to achieving what shareholders want, which, in most cases, but not always, is wealth maximization.

Yes, maximizing shareholder value can come at the cost of destroying many other things that are good in the world but that's how markets work. To change that, we need to change what our democratically elected governments allow for-profit corporations to do or not do.

Unless potential shareholders see a possibility of high return, they wouldn't invest in a business. Without an investment, a business wouldn't get off the ground. Hence, an entrepreneur has no choice but to start thinking like a shareholder, who is unemotional about a business but is solely focused on the logic of generating outsized financial returns.

The focus on maximizing shareholder value will eventually make you do things that you may not be naturally inclined to do. So, even if you are kind-hearted and have good intentions in mind, the expectation of profit maximization for shareholders will ultimately be the biggest influence on your decisions.

That is why, starting a business to do good or change the world is kind of a self-deception if you clearly understand why businesses exist under our current capitalist system. If 'maximizing shareholder value' sounds unsavory or too shallow, you are better off not starting a for-profit company.

> **Remember:** good entrepreneurs do not hesitate in taking (emotionally) hard decisions because they are perfectly aligned with what investors and shareholders want, which is often wealth maximization.

PART 11

EXECUTING WELL

WHAT KILLS STARTUPS IS THE LACK OF FEEDBACK

A startup is like a hypothesis inside an entrepreneur's head and the entire point of the startup journey is to know whether it's true or false. This search for what's true is important because, if found, it's worth a lot of money.

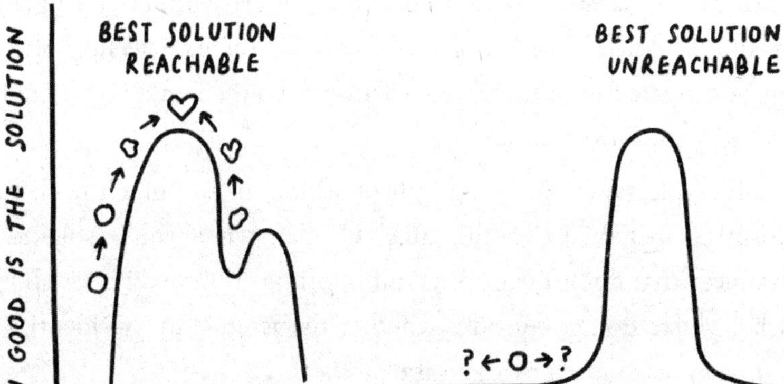

Feedback—both positive or negative—forces you to iterate towards a better product

Entrepreneurs thrive on feedback from users. Each bit of feedback—even if it is negative—will guide where to look. In fact, negative feedback is a clear indicator that you have identified the right problem, but perhaps the specific solution that you came up with is lacking.

You should embrace negative feedback because it shows that customers are at least paying attention. What you should fear is silence. If no feedback is coming your way or prospects are not replying to emails, or users are dropping off from the product without telling you why, then there's simply no way for you to iterate.

Radio silence from the market makes it difficult to iterate. But, there's a psychological impact of working in the dark too. It's extremely demotivating to keep putting effort without getting any feedback. At least with negative feedback, there's a feeling of the right struggle. But if there's no reaction from the market, you might just give up in frustration.

This silence might be a result of asking for too much from the customer before delivering value. Or that when you're solving a problem that doesn't exist or is unimportant. If nobody cares about what you're doing, consider whether the issue is in the identified problem or your approach in the market.

Since success depends on knowing the direction that leads to success, it is important to maximize the rate of feedback in the early days. Many entrepreneurs tend to keep their idea secret and spend a ton of time building the perfect product which gets no reaction from the market when it is launched.

Instead of keeping secrets, you should share what you're building openly and engage with potential customers from day one so that you start getting tiny doses of feedback every day. This will enable you to identify a clear direction for progress, creating a positive feedback cycle of motivation to progress even further.

> **Remember:** nothing succeeds like the feeling that you're succeeding.

STUDY YOUR MOST SUCCESSFUL CUSTOMERS TO SET YOUR DIRECTION

Once you launch a product, setting its future direction is actually really simple:

- Study your most successful customers in detail.
- Know *why* they are more successful than other customers. Ask: how are they using the product that others aren't?
- Take those lessons and tweak your product in a way that nudges all other customers to be a bit more like the most successful ones.
- Refine your pitch to highlight aspects of your products that your most successful customers get value from.

Your most successful customers are the ones who have by themselves discovered the use cases of your products that give them an enormous benefit. When your customers are working so hard to derive value from your product, your job boils down to observing them. Interview successful customers and figure out how to make their valued use cases explicit in your product to other less successful customers.

It is also possible that some customers discover a use case of your product that you never designed your product for. When you discover these accidental use cases, highlight them in your marketing pitch to tap into entirely new customer types.

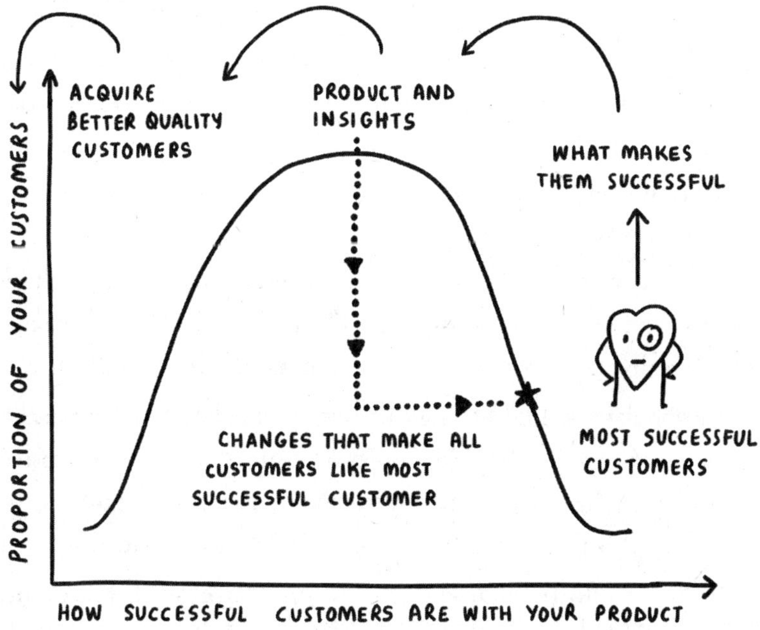

Your most successful customers are probably also your most underutilized resource

The definition of 'successful customers' differs from business to business, but a good proxy is the time spent using your products. You need to find customers whose actions (not words) reveal that they're getting a lot of benefits from your product. Use analytics to figure out who is in love with your products and then interview them to know why. But while interviewing customers, remember to not ask 'what do you like most about the product'.

Rather, ask them to recall how they use your product. Your customers cannot give you insights on use cases, they can only supply the raw data. Instead, you need to infer from repeated patterns and derive insights into why some take that benefit while the rest of the customers don't.

An example of what studying successful customers can lead to is Facebook's timeline feature. Before the timeline came along, Facebook users had to visit their friends' profiles to check what changed in their lives. Like most behaviours, this one was also different for each user. Some rarely checked user profiles but others did it obsessively.

By discovering such obsessive behaviour of people checking friends' profiles several times a day, Facebook realized that perhaps people really like to know what's happening in other people's lives.

Facebook took this learning and experimented with automatically surfacing changes in people's profiles on a timeline. It was a massive success, one that increased time spent on Facebook significantly, and today, it is the central feature of all social media platforms.

Of course, the timeline experiment could have failed. The point, however, is that new product feature ideation didn't happen in a vacuum. Facebook mined for outlier behaviours in its user base to discover an obsessive use case, which was then productized for the rest of the users.

> **Remember:** your most successful customers will use your product in ways you never designed it for. Your job is to polish these 'newly discovered' use cases and offer them to the entire market.

YOUR NORTH STAR METRIC SHOULD BE A LEADING INDICATOR OF PROFITS

Kodak, Toys R Us and Blockbuster were market-leading companies with hundreds of millions of dollars in revenue at their peak. During their heyday, nobody could have predicted that they would one day go bankrupt. Yet, they did and gave us a real world case for why revenue or profit is exactly the wrong metric when it comes to predicting the future of a company.

Financial metrics are, of course, important from an accounting point of view. But they are strictly backward-looking. They tell you

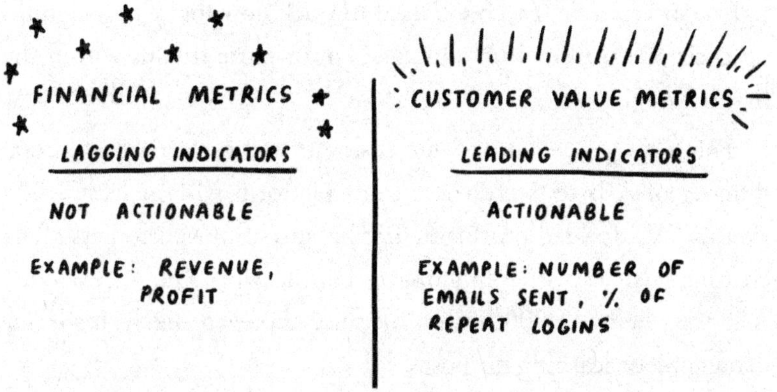

Always pay attention to what's actionable

how the company has performed in the past but have very little actionable information for the future. As an entrepreneur, you need to pay attention to where future growth will come from, not simply review the past growth. That's the job of the accountants.

So, if not financial metrics, what metrics should you—the entrepreneur—pay attention to?

The short answer is customer value metrics. These are the metrics that track in real time the value your customers are deriving from your products or services. Essentially, customer value metrics are the numbers that are good proxies for value creation in the world by your product. Another way to look at these metrics is to figure out what numbers are good leading indicators for lagging financial metrics such as revenue or profit.

It's easy to get customer value metrics wrong. Many startups track user signups or daily active users, not realizing that a customer signing up for the service hasn't yet derived any value from the product. Good indicators for customer value happen downstream of the signup process, and that's why they're also very hard to get right. For example, Facebook used to track how many new signups on their platform end up adding seven or more friends within the first ten days.

For VWO, my startup, our customer value metric is the total number of A/B tests created on our platform with at least 1,000 visitors. We decided on this metric because if our customers aren't creating A/B tests, they're going to churn. Moreover, we excluded A/B tests below 1,000 visitors because those are likely made for debugging or learning purposes.

We validated our customer value metric by segmenting our churn rate by it and, sure enough, customers with higher customer value metrics had lower churn and higher lifetime revenue.

To ensure you're looking towards the future, not the past, find your own customer value metrics and then track them obsessively. If you are able to discover metrics that are predictive of your revenue or profits, then you have a magic tool to be able to influence future financial metrics in a very predictable way by simply focusing on increasing that number.

> **Remember:** make customer value metrics your north star, and financial metrics will automatically be taken care of.

PART 12

BUILDING A TEAM

YOUR TEAM'S CULTURE IS DEFINED BY YOUR BEHAVIOUR, NOT YOUR WORDS

Imagine you're the founder of a startup project (it could be a company, a non-profit, a religion or even a country). You have a weird habit: you like to come to the office by noon and stay late (say until 8 p.m.). You hire your first employee, and on the first day he arrives at the office at 9 a.m. (just like he did in his previous job).

How you behave today is how your team will behave tomorrow

The empty office seems odd to him, and it becomes odder still when he sees you stroll by in the office during his lunchtime. In the evening, since it's the first day of his job, he waits for you to leave but the entire time, you are happily busy on your laptop. You leave the office by 9 p.m. and a couple of minutes after you, the new hire leaves. Thinking of his first day as a fluke, the new employee comes in early again tomorrow but the same thing repeats.

As you can guess, new employees usually don't confront their bosses in the early days, so they end up adapting themselves to their bosses' weird habits. When another new employee joins, she now sees two people working from noon to 8 p.m. So the pressure is even more to conform. As the team grows, for new hires, the situation gradually starts looking like a cult to the outsiders (a group of people who work from noon to 8 p.m.).

As more people join and as more time passes, it becomes harder for anyone (including the old members) to change these joint habits. This becomes the company's culture. Continuing with the previous example, imagine that the company has now grown to 100 people and the CEO has had a change of heart. He declares that the noon timing is no longer okay and that everyone has to come to the office by sharp nine in the morning. How do you think this proposal will be perceived by the company?

The criticism will likely be one among these: 'our culture is changing', 'it's not like the old days anymore' and 'here are 99 reasons why noon to 8 p.m. is the best timing'. People don't like to change the habits that they've adopted over time.

If the CEO himself faces resistance to changing these culturally ingrained joint habits, imagine how difficult will it be for anyone else (including new joiners) to try doing the same?

Organizations are, therefore, habit amplifying machines. What is amplified in an organization is not just weird habits, but all habits (good or bad) of the initial founding team. Do founders like to read? They'll attract, retain and encourage people to read. Soon enough, reading books becomes part of the culture.

In America's case, since their founding fathers gave great emphasis on freedom of gun-owning, changing it now is political suicide for US politicians. Similarly, China's totalitarianism that started with Mao Zedong's rule reflects today in the government's tracking and rating of its citizens. Apple's maniacal focus on design continues even after the death of Steve Jobs.

When people ask why can't China now adopt democracy given that they have everything else going for them, they're missing the point that an organization resists change in its collective culture. Which is nothing but shared behaviours and habits reinforced over the course of time.

Cultures do change but require either a million tiny nudges or a full-blown revolution. In the default case, culture, once established, resists change.

> **Remember:** new employees observe previous employees to guess what's okay to do and what's not okay. And you—the founder—are the first employee.

DON'T HIRE FOR ROLES, HIRE FOR A CHANGE

It's easy to hire people. You think of what's the next bottleneck in your organization's growth and hire a role to fill that bottleneck. Typically, this involves coming up with a job description (which is often copy-pasted from elsewhere), announcing the job opening, and then interviewing candidates.

Sounds easy, isn't it?

Hiring people is the easy bit—there are enough candidates waiting to be hired. But the challenge lies in hiring someone who

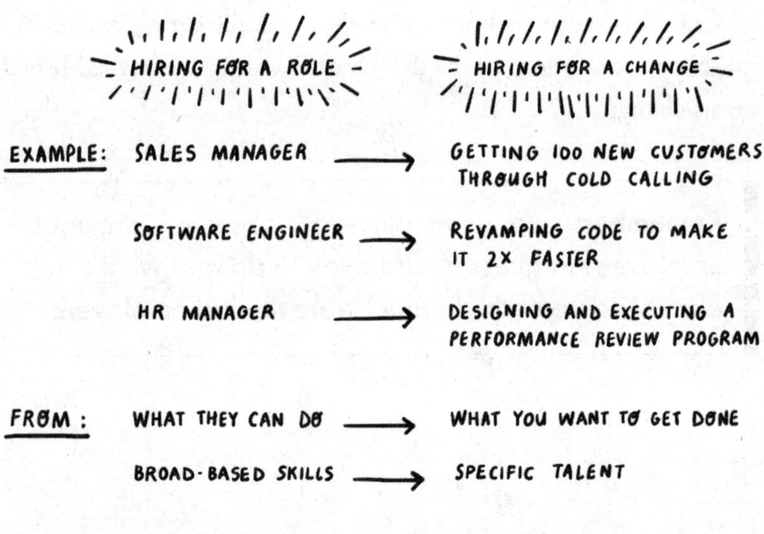

Ask yourself: what change do I want in the company?

emerges as a star performer, contributing significantly to your company's growth.

Why is hiring star performers difficult? It's often because founders don't spend enough time trying to get clarity within their heads on what star performance means for *their* organizations. They usually hire for generic roles like "Sales Manager" or "Software Engineer", and only a small percentage of such generic hires end up being good at precisely the thing that the organization needs at the moment.

What a specific 'sales manager' or a 'data scientist' does varies significantly from person to person. Labels can capture only so much.

So, before hiring, you must know what precise change a new hire is expected to bring to the organization in the next twelve–eighteen months. No business needs 'software engineers'; what it needs is instead 'developing and releasing a bug-free feature to customers, to increase revenue'.

This clarity on what specific tasks a new hire is expected to excel at in order to be called a star performer helps in multiple ways. It gives clarity in interviews about whether an otherwise motivated person is skilled enough to bring about the impact that your organization wants. It also helps in communicating clear expectations to the candidate so there are fewer surprises later on.

Importantly, this clarity helps smoothly onboarding a new hire. On day one, the candidate knows what task she is brought into the company for, and hence, rather than going through generic training and onboarding, the candidate applies herself to getting up to speed on the specific things which she is hired for, which ultimately benefits the company.

So, before you hire, assume you've already hired the perfect candidate and visualize what specific changes has she brought into your organization's growth. Then go ahead and hire the person who can bring about those changes. Whether you call that person a software engineer or a ninja is beside the question. The important thing is to know clearly what you are hiring the person for.

> **Remember:** before you hire, know what specific change you want in your organization.

THE NUMBER ONE JOB OF A FOUNDER IS TO COMMUNICATE CLARITY

In the very early stages, when there are few people in the startup, only a handful of projects are running parallelly at any point in time. The founder typically knows how such projects connect with and reinforce each other to produce a combined output that's more than the sum of all individual projects.

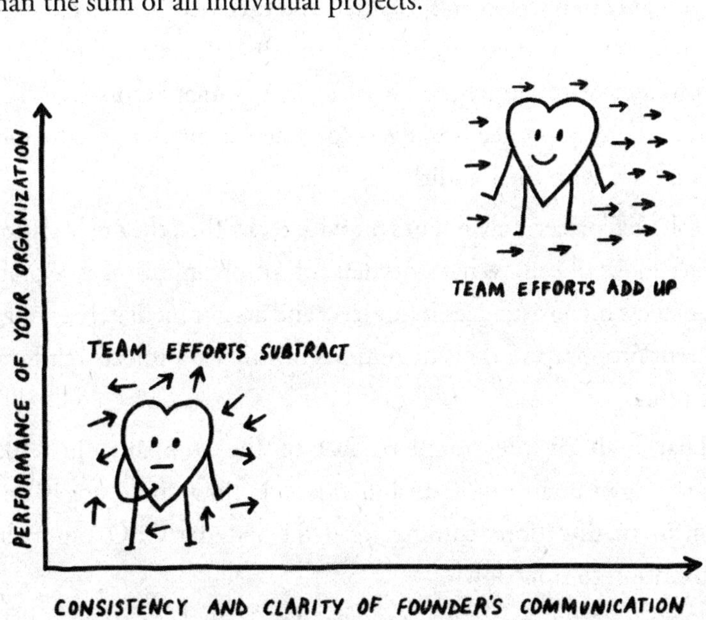

Organizations amplify the directions coming from the top

As an extreme example of this, consider the organization when it is just one person: the founder. This person has the luxury of high-bandwidth communication between different concepts sitting in his/her brain. The product manager, the marketer, the developer, the designer—all are sitting in the same brain of the founder, and hence, alignment of all actions is a natural outcome. Whenever there's an impulse in one part of the brain (like launching a new feature), another part of the brain immediately pitches in to prevent it from getting misaligned (like wondering 'how will this feature sell?').

As an organization grows, founders typically get frustrated and overwhelmed by their inability to manage and control various projects that different people are undertaking. Individually, these projects are often well conceptualized and executed. However, taken together, many of these projects fail to reinforce each other. What the product team launches, the sales team is unable to sell. When the marketing team needs budgets for a new campaign, the finance team is busy with their audit.

If all such projects are not in sync with each other, the organization doesn't move ahead. What's needed for an organization is a brain that detects inconsistencies in projects and acts immediately to align different proposals so that the outputs from most projects reinforce each other.

That brain is the founder/CEO of the company. Just like when a foggy brain causes an individual to slow down, foggy and inconsistent directions coming from the founder/CEO cause the organization to slow down.

This is why your number one job as the founder/CEO needs to consistently and repeatedly communicate clarity to everyone in the organization. Of course, before you do that, it's important to have clarity in the first place. You cannot give clarity to your team if you don't have it.

Imagine a new marketing person joins your team, and you tell him that he needs to increase signups on the website. There are so many different ways of increasing signups. What if the marketer increases signups that are of no use to the sales team? What if the marketer demands a budget for this that you can't afford?

So, to get the job done in the right manner, you need to know all these constraints. Put in the effort to know how all projects in the organization connect to a bigger plan (some people call this strategy).

Once you have clarity, communicate it to the team and ensure people have understood the context as you intended it to be. This is not micromanagement. It's micro-communication, and it ensures everyone in your organization knows your assumptions clearly.

Yes, this requires a lot of effort and may make you wonder how you're going to get anything else done in the organization. But the alternative is the opportunity cost of doing wrong projects and spending more effort later in correcting all the damage.

> **Remember:** the most important job that founders/ CEOs have is to keep aligning their teams all the time. For the rest of the jobs, they should hire people who can do the job better than them.

AIM TO BE A CULT BY HIRING PEOPLE WHO OBSESS ABOUT THE SAME THINGS

Many mainstream trends start as a cult, when a small group of people start obsessing about an idea that nobody else cares for. Veganism was once a cult, and so was the idea of the US as a country. Science began as a cult when the Royal Society of London adopted 'Nullius in verba' as its motto. By asking its members to

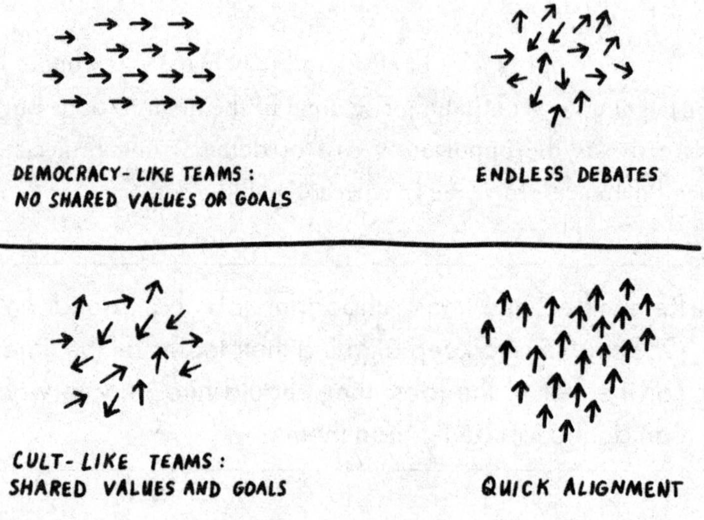

Hire people who share similar values

take nobody's word of it, the Royal Society became attractive to certain people and extremely unattractive to other people. This cohesion of views is what laid the foundation of modern science's growth from a startup to a major force in the world.

Startups should aim to be like cults because effective communication is almost impossible between people with different values. If you are someone who believes in taking nobody's word for it and someone else has unquestionable faith in God, no matter how hard you both try, your communication is going to break at some point on matters of faith.

In the real world, democracy is great. It ensures that after a lot of effort and tons of debates, people can settle for a compromise. But startups are not countries. Startups need to grow fast, and for that, they need to execute fast.

If your early team isn't convinced that the world will be a worse place without your products, they simply won't put the passion and energy required to make it happen. As an entrepreneur, you need to hire people who share the very same crazy view about reality as you. Of course, all of you could be wrong together (and that's why most startups fail). But you'll at least spend your energy on customers and the market discovering whether your problem–solution pair is valuable or not, and not in internal 'alignment'.

Note that as a startup grows bigger, the cost of failures rises, and hence, alignment to find correct answers, even after cost of speed, becomes important. But for startups failing is default, and being a cult helps in having a shot at discovering something valuable that the mainstream hasn't caught on to yet.

HOW DO YOU BUILD A CULT-LIKE TEAM?

People tend to hire people like them. But, if you hire someone with different values, they'll hire people like themselves. Pretty soon, your entire company will be a heterogeneous group that consumes all your energy towards getting everything aligned.

This is why you should pay attention to the values of the person you're hiring. For example, it'll be disastrous for a startup to hire a genius who's rude when everyone else in the team values respectful interactions (or vice versa). In this scenario, as a founder, you'll find your energy consumed by telling the genius to tone down while telling others to be okay with a bit of 'directness'.

This is a big waste of time and energy. You'll eventually start hating getting your team to 'align'.

So, during interviews, focus on asking questions that reveal a person's worldview and see that it aligns with your worldview.

The beauty of hiring for similar values early on is that after a while, it becomes self-sustaining. If the early team is homogenous, they will keep on hiring people who're like them. So, as your company scales, you have to worry less about this. In fact, because of homogeneity, as the company grows, not having enough dissenting views becomes a problem. Cults become detrimental in the company's growth later on, but early on, they're absolutely required.

WHAT ABOUT DIVERSITY?

I'm not advocating for hiring clones. Diversity is useful, but only as long as it's the diversity of the right kind. Every one gains tremendously from the diversity of experiences in the team as lived experiences are useful data points. What someone else knows that you don't is valuable.

So, a good recipe for a team is having people with different experiences but similar values.

However, this combination is hard to find because people's experiences shape their values. So if you're able to find someone with different experiences than you but with a very similar worldview, hire them. But beware of championing diversity without understanding what kind of diversity you are creating.

Remember: when speed is everything for a startup, cult-like teams are faster than democratic teams.

YOUR COMPANY'S ORGANIZATION CHART IS MORE IMPORTANT THAN YOU THINK

Right from the start, you should plan for what arrangement of people will be most suitable for delivering the goals of your company and what arrangement may be required about a year after. It's important that you, the founder, obsess over organization design because no one else would do this thinking.

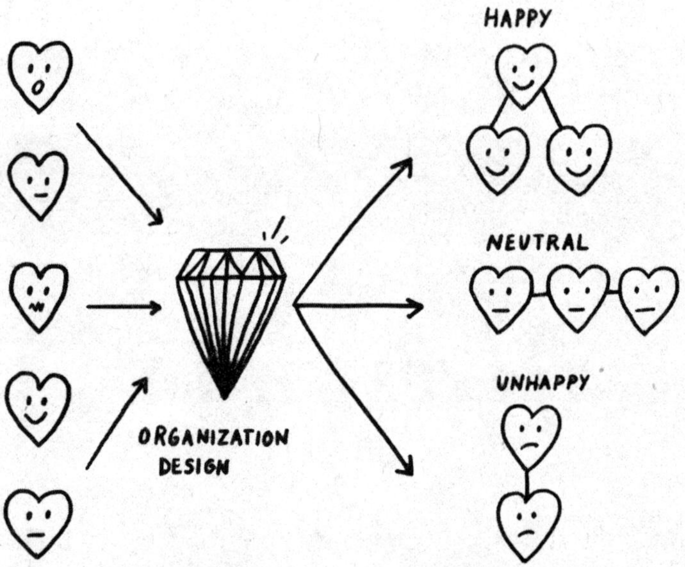

Same people in different arrangements lead to different levels of satisfaction and success

No employee will come to you and ask to be fired, so you can hire a specialist instead. Only an entrepreneur can take this call proactively.

Organization design is simply what roles should be there in the company and how those roles are related to each other. Many entrepreneurs and CEOs follow industry norms in hiring, and so their organization chart takes a standard shape that's indistinguishable from their competitors'.

That's inefficient because your company has an essentially unique strategy (I hope!) and hence deserves a unique organization design that implements that strategy effectively.

In some cases, organization design happens by accident because there's no well-thought strategy. So, a prerequisite for doing organization design is developing clarity on strategy. Because if there's no clarity you must know how you will win before deciding who should be on which team, then whatever organization chart you have will automatically start determining what your strategy is.

HOW TO DESIGN YOUR ORGANIZATION CHART

To be a good organization designer, you have to be a good psychologist. You have to first learn what conditions bring out stellar performances in individuals and then design a structure where people can find themselves in such conditions.

Here are some common mistakes that entrepreneurs make while designing their organization:

- *Underinvesting in specialist roles.* It's true that you don't realize how much better a job can be done until you've seen someone do it 10x better. This means that for each role in your company, there are people who can do parts or the entirety of it 10x better than your current generalist team. You don't need a good marketer; what you need is someone who's killer at search engine advertising for your industry. You don't need a frontend engineer; what you need is a frontend performance engineer who can speed up your app 10x, considerably impacting user satisfaction. If there's a job worth doing well (from the perspective of your strategy), hire a specialist.

- *Having quality functions report into quantity functions.* Functions such as QA and development should always be parallel in the organization chart and not report to one another. If you report quality-oriented functions into quantity-oriented ones, quality will suffer. If you report quantity into quality, speed will suffer.
- *Having long-term initiatives report into people accountable for the short term.* This is the reason big organizations often cannot innovate when it comes to completely new initiatives. For people who're tasked with short-term targets, long-term initiatives are a distraction because at the start, they're simply too small or too risky to get meaningful attention or resources. Since such people's performance is measured on short-term targets, the big and the scaled-up is where their interest goes. This lack of early nurturing causes long-term initiatives to fail early, creating a vicious cycle of stagnation. To solve this, long-term initiatives (such as strategy, R&D lab or brand building) need to be put into a separate place in the organization chart (perhaps under a leader who reports directly to the entrepreneur/CEO).

- *Not eliminating outdated roles and functions fast enough.* The organization chart should change as the strategy of the organization changes, which happens automatically as the company grows. The chart implements the strategy, so not changing it frequently means your company will keep attempting to grow via the old ways. So, one of the key jobs of the entrepreneur/CEO and the board is to frequently assess if the organization chart is aligned to the strategy.
- *Promoting high performers to be managers and leaders.* This is super-hard to avoid in reality, but when star performers get promoted, the organization gets damaged twice: one, the person who does the specialist job well isn't there to perform it, second, now you have a manager who is probably a mediocre one (when you could have gotten an experienced manager). If you promote your best performers to managers, ultimately your organization will be full of mediocre managers.
- Too often, organization charts revolve around the availability of people (and the fear of losing high performers). The right way, however, is to be clear of what roles exist in the chart and what types of people will perform those roles best. Don't fit roles into people, fit people into roles.

> **Remember**: organization design should be a deliberate exercise, as it is what'll determine if your strategy gets executed well or not. Most roles in history didn't exist until someone thought of it. So if you have to invent a role, you should.

YOU'RE PROBABLY NOT A GOOD LEADER (BECAUSE BEING THAT IS HARD)

Most entrepreneurs believe that they're good leaders because their team does what they ask them to do.

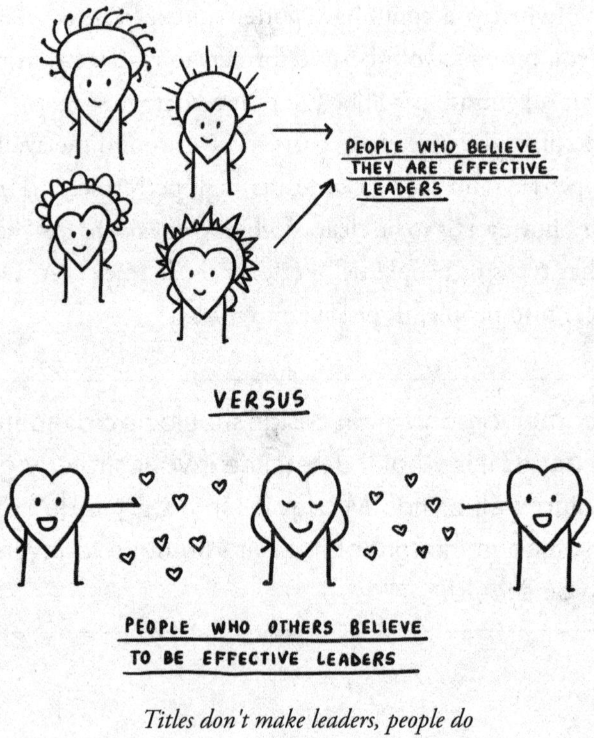

Titles don't make leaders, people do

But that's not leadership—that's simply people working because you're paying them money to work.

There's a big difference between compliance and commitment. Entrepreneurs often get compliance with their decisions, but they end up assuming that they're getting commitment.

Leadership is difficult because human nature evolved in a very different setting (hunting and gathering) than what a modern company is. During the course of evolution, we evolved gut-level like or dislike reactions to people that still exist in us today.

This makes the job of a leader tricky because she has to focus on the quality of work and get the job done, despite whether she personally likes the person or not. Also, the leader has to somehow navigate people's widely different emotions, desires, and personalities and make them work together to deliver an organization's goals.

Now, that's tough.

What makes an effective leader is hard to summarize, but let's give it a try. Here are the ten hard steps to become a good leader:

1. Everyone wants to progress, but only leaders are willing to sacrifice for it.

We all know what's good for us: exercising regularly, eating healthy food, not smoking and meditating. Yet, how many of us have the willpower to follow through?

Wanting and really wanting are two different things. Really wanting requires sacrificing short-term happiness for long-term success. You know this already, but you also know that the common wisdom is hard to follow through. We all fall into temptations decided by our today's mood.

Leadership requires not falling into today's temptation and putting in long hours when you least feel like doing it. To be a leader is to sacrifice today for tomorrow.

2. Leaders look up, while non-leaders look sideways.

When we're young in our careers, it's natural to bond with co-workers and peers of similar age. And just like college, it's easy to huddle up with work friends and get into a comfort zone.

We are a sum of people we spend time with. If your standards of work quality and effort are set by your peer group, you'll progress slowly. To be a leader is to always set your standards to what people much better than yourself have (and not the standards that people like you in your peer group have).

3. Leaders select themselves in roles of leadership.

It's a myth that people are promoted to leadership positions. Leaders don't wait for an official leadership position or title. They simply start behaving like leaders wherever they are, and then the organization simply gives them a leadership title to recognize what they were doing anyway.

As the name implies, leadership means leading the organization and not just following instructions (of investors, if you're an entrepreneur, or manager, if you're an employee).

Your chosen direction could be wrong, so you may gravitate towards playing it safe and only doing what is explicitly asked. But that's not leadership. To lead is to take the risk of being entirely wrong.

4. Leaders make themselves dependable and indispensable.

Different people have different definitions of 'work'. For most people, 'work' is a set of activities they need to perform to make a salary. For leaders, 'work' is more personal, as they put their soul into their work. Since they have high standards, they take it personally when they fail to deliver. They know it's upon them to work harder if the deadlines are tight, or when they're asked to do the impossible.

Irrespective of what project is given to them, a leader rarely externalizes failure on someone else. Leaders never make excuses. Never. They always take it upon themselves to do whatever it takes to get stuff done.

While others are working, leaders are delivering. The tenacity and stubbornness to deliver good results make them dependable. Since the organization knows they always deliver, they're given more responsibilities, and they get pulled into the most important projects. Leaders consistently prove their ability to deliver, and that's how they become indispensable.

5. Discipline is a superpower and leaders know that.

To be disciplined is to always show up on time, taking copious notes in discussions, delivering before deadlines, doing regular and consistent follow-ups, and most importantly, keeping your promises. Sounds simple, but many 'leaders' fail at these basics spectacularly. Their team gradually realizes this and slowly sloppiness becomes the norm.

For people early in their careers, being disciplined is probably the number one predictor of their success. (And it's also unfortunate how few know that it is so important).

As they say, the secret to life is simply showing up.

6. Leaders are unpopular among their peers because they work hard, know more and deliver regularly.

It's counter-intuitive, but leaders quickly become unpopular in their peer group because they're just so much better at what they do. This growing unpopularity makes many would-be leaders uncomfortable, and they start changing their behaviour to gain approval from their peer group.

Leaders who break through swallow the bitter pill and do what's right for their growth. A group of non-leaders is like friends—they comfort each other. A group of leaders is like a soccer club—they know that their lack of performance cannot be justified because someone else on their team is not performing. They understand that when the next season comes, it'll be their performance that'll count first, and only then the performance of the team they belong to.

7. Leaders are intimidating because they're masters of their craft.

When you talk to leaders, they're capable of intimidating you because they know so much about their field. All great leaders are functional experts. You put them against a peer in the same function, and they'll know more both in depth and in breadth.

This almost PhD-level mastery of their field requires long stretches of tinkering, reading and thinking. And the interesting part is: nobody asks them to master their craft. It's easy for them to be good at what they do, but they're not satisfied with that: they want to become great at what they do.

Non-leaders have a 'fixed' mindset and accept their fate of learning ability or IQ. Leaders have a 'growth' mindset, and that makes them put in additional hours every day required to master their craft. (The extra hours require sacrifice, but that's requirement number one for leadership.)

8. Leaders lift the entire boat, and not just themselves.

Leaders are independent but not individualistic.

People who're individualistic in nature hit a ceiling in their career because as they grow, they find their job transforms from doing great work by themselves to helping others do great work. But because bright young people are driven to succeed, they start competing with the very people they're expected to help.

To be a leader is not to be competitive. It's to be great at what you do and proactively go around in the organization asking everyone, 'Hey, how can I help you?' Taking the analogy of a football club, this means a star player knows that to be successful, s/he has to perform his/her best and coach/encourage/mentor fellow players to perform their best.

The selfish path to greatness is to help others become great.

9. Leaders are firm in their resolve but never disrespect.

One of the hardest parts of becoming a leader is to learn how to be firm and direct, without being disrespectful. It's easy to tilt in either direction: you can be nice and accommodating, but get pulled down by the tendency to please others. Or you can be rude and tell others how pathetic they are.

Neither of these is okay. What's required is a fine balance where you're direct but respectful. Ill-mannered people that perform spectacularly hit a ceiling in their career.

So do really sweet people who get rolled over by lack of performance by their peers or team.

10. Leadership is hard, so it's okay to not aim for leadership, but it's not okay to whine.

Leadership is glamorous as leaders get fat salaries prestige, and juicy projects. But it's also not meant for everyone.

To summarize, leadership requires *all* the attributes below:

- Putting in long hours at work
- Being paranoid about discipline
- Moving mountains to deliver impossible asks
- Being okay when other people dislike you
- Offering to help everyone around
- Mastering your craft inside-out
- Proactively and continuously tinkering, learning and thinking
- Taking risks by doing more than what's asked
- Starting uncomfortable conversations but not losing temper

You miss an attribute, and you toss away your chances at leadership. This means leadership requires deliberate effort over long stretches of time. It's a process that never ends because there's always a better leader out there who can do what you do better and faster.

> **Remember**: choose leadership as a career choice only if you're willing to work for it. It's okay to select a comfortable career, too, as long as it's a deliberate choice. What's not okay is wanting to progress but not willing to sacrifice for that progress. Sorry, you can't have your cake and eat it too.

PART 13

THINKING CLEARLY

ALWAYS SEEK DISCONFIRMATORY EVIDENCE

Thinking is expensive for an animal—our brain consumes almost 20 per cent of the energy of the body (even at rest). Hence, one brain takes whatever shortcuts it can to do less deliberate thinking (that requires more energy) and more automatic thinking (that requires less energy).

There's another name for such automatic thinking: cognitive bias.

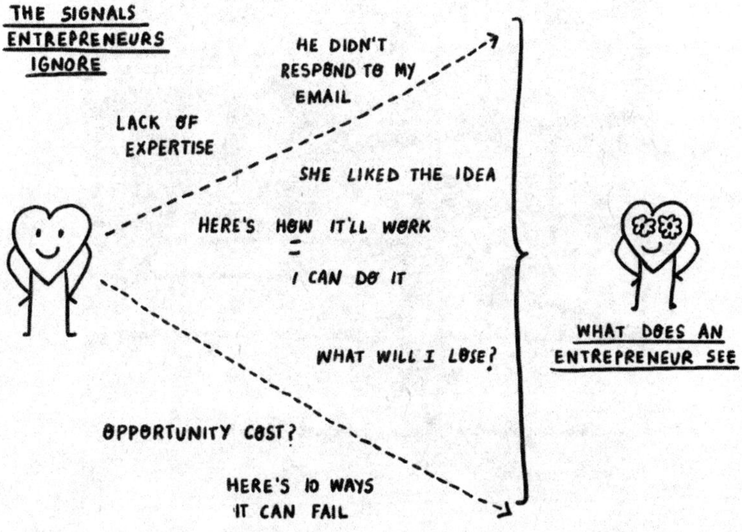

Confirmation and confidence bias: the two cognitive biases that kill most startups

The word bias is used here because our preprogrammed ways of thinking bias us towards paying more attention to certain information at the expense of ignoring other information. So, *cognitive biases are systematic errors in viewing the world.* They are very hard to correct because you literally see the world through a lens that's painted with cognitive biases.

For example, take a look at the following image:[1]

What if I tell you that both monsters are of equal sizes? Unless you've seen this illusion before, this information is likely a surprise to you because 'obviously, one is bigger than the other'. But that isn't so. Measure both monsters with a scale, and you'll know.

The reason one monster appears much larger than the other is because our brain likes taking shortcuts. For this image, your brain takes cues from the perspectival depth in the image to conclude relative size. This shortcut works really well in reality like when seeing mountains at a distance, but like in this image, it can backfire.

Particularly relevant to entrepreneurs are two cognitive biases: confirmation bias and confidence bias.

Confirmation bias leads you to overweight information that aligns to your beliefs while underweighting disconfirmatory information. And confidence bias leads you to overestimate your abilities while ignoring your weak areas. These biases help us make important decisions since, if we always remain doubtful of our beliefs, we may never be able to decide. And since we can't survive without taking decisions, these biases evolved to reduce doubt. So, biases are evolved shortcuts that helped our survival chases during the course of human evolution. But in today's context they can backfire.

Even though confidence is a necessary ingredient in entrepreneurial ventures, it's also the major reason for failure. Due to confirmation bias, you would tend to select all the positive evidence towards your idea and because of confidence bias, you would overweight your ability to execute on that idea (while underweighting risks or opportunity costs). Taking informed risk is great but taking blind risk is not.

This is why you must consciously strive to expand his perspective to include disconfirmatory evidence. This can be done by asking or thinking about specific ways in which an idea can fail, or by making a pros-and-cons list. Many successful entrepreneurs spend disproportionately more time focusing specifically on potential reasons for failure because they know their mind will automatically rush to potential reasons for success. The pros of an idea come easily and naturally, and that is why the focus should be to find the cons. So, as a rule, you must always list evidence and reasons for potential failure (including an honest assessment of one's risks and opportunity costs).

Cognitive biases are a double-edged sword because the confidence that you get from believing that your idea will work is needed to make it work. The decoupling of entrepreneurial energy and knowledge of reality of one's ideas and abilities is rare.

> **Remember:** overconfidence gives energy, but also lets people spend years solving make-believe problems that nobody has. Be skeptical. Whenever you're feeling too excited about something, always seek disconfirmatory evidence.

NEVER ASK YOUR FRIENDS OR FAMILY IF THEY LIKE YOUR IDEA

People are generally nice in person. You'd know this if you have ever gone to parties where everyone is super nice to others, but as soon as the party is over, they start gossiping about the ones who've left. Very rarely would anyone tell a person at the party that they look like a clown (while often thinking the same in their head).

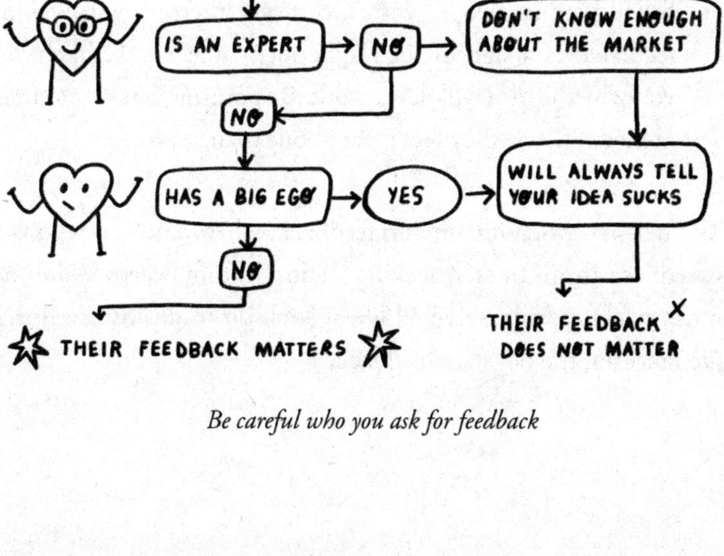

Be careful who you ask for feedback

This tendency of people to not honestly tell what they have in mind misleads entrepreneurs when they seek feedback on their idea. Even if the idea you pitch is obviously flawed, in general, no one will tell that to your face. This means, you rarely get to hear why your idea sucks.

Combine this tendency of people to avoid giving negative feedback with the tendency of listeners to seek confirmatory feedback and you have the perfect recipe for delusion. The problem worsens when feedback is sought from close ones. Friends and family will never want to offend you, so they would go to great lengths to justify why your idea is a bright one. The more a person is close to you, the more the person will rationalize. But what you want is truth, not fabrications.

There are two more problems with asking for feedback from non-experts (such as family or friends).

- First, a common person neither knows enough about startups, nor knows enough about a specific market to be able to give you useful insights.
- Second, some people with a big ego interpret you seeking feedback as a sign of their superiority and would likely tell you why the idea will never work. By pointing out (sometimes obvious) flaws, they feel great about themselves.

So, net-net, when it comes to feedback, what matters is who you ask feedback from. In fact, seeking feedback from everyone around you can backfire because you'll likely latch on to positive feedback while ignoring the negative feedback.

You want to seek feedback from someone who is honest, and is an expert in your target market and doesn't have a big ego.

Such people are rare, but that's why you have to be selective in deciding whose feedback to act upon.

> **Remember:** not all feedback is worthwhile. It matters who you ask feedback from.

ASK PEOPLE WHAT THEY DID, NOT WHAT THEY WILL DO

When it comes to our life and decisions, we're optimistic rationalizers. Every new year's eve, we make resolutions that are grounded in perfectly valid reasons—reducing weight, quitting cigarettes, reading more books, and so on. If someone asks why we want to read books, we can confidently blurt out that it will expand our worldview.

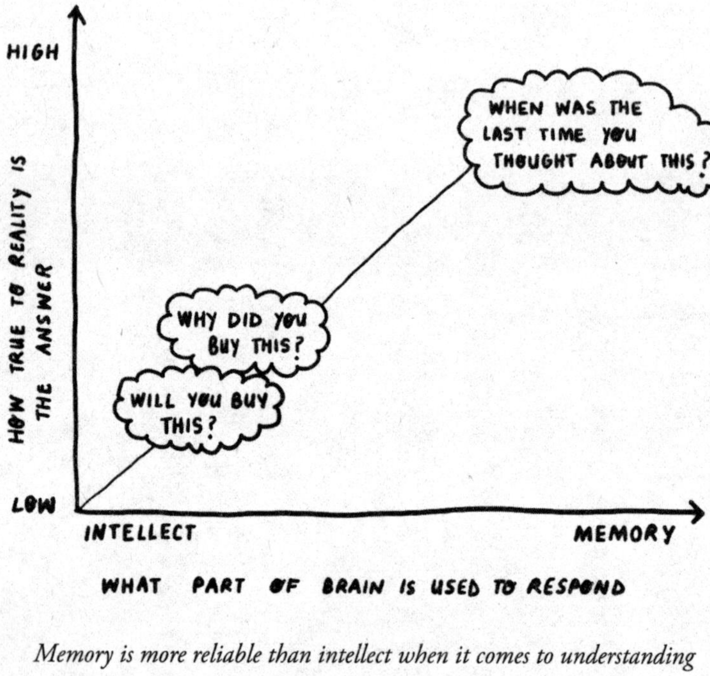

Memory is more reliable than intellect when it comes to understanding customer behaviour

Fast-forward a couple of weeks in the new year, and we're often back to our old ways. It's spectacular that even when we quit our yearly resolution within weeks, we always have good reasons for why we abandoned our goals. (We rarely acknowledge that we are lazy or are addicted to cigarettes.)

This tendency of people to provide well–thought-out reasons to justify their behaviour easily misleads entrepreneurs who go around asking, 'If I build this, will you buy it?'

If you put people under the spotlight of this question, they will say something that makes sense. Nobody wants to appear like a fool. However, the key question is if they'll act the same way too when you're not around.

Asking people to justify their purchases or to imagine whether they will make a specific purchase is a useless exercise. If someone has purchased a TV of a specific brand, and you ask them why they purchased it, you'll likely get a battery of reasons. People want to appear rational decision makers, so they will cite price, quality, technology or other dimensions as criteria.

However, the truth may be that it was an impulse purchase because of a discount during a trip to a mall.

Actually, it's not like people lie on purpose. Rather, our brains have evolved to supply justifications for our actions. So asking someone to rely on reasoning and intellect is a sure shot way of getting fabricated answers.

Rather than asking people to use their imagination, a much better way to interview is to probe their actual past behaviour. That way, you're more likely to get a truer picture of how they behave (smoking several cigarettes every day) rather than getting reasons for how they want to behave (quitting the habit).

People say all sorts of things to comfort themselves and others while they happily go about doing something else. As an entrepreneur, you're interested in what they actually do, not what they say.

If someone is truly interested in quitting cigarettes, you'll see this in their behaviour when you probe and nudge them about their attempts to quit. If it is their burning desire to quit cigarettes, and they haven't been able to do it, they will remember many such attempts with clarity. In contrast, if quitting is just someone's idle desire, they'll fumble and not clearly remember when was the last time they seriously attempted quitting cigarettes.

A practical tip on orienting people to rely on their memory: Ask them to imagine a documentary being shot on their life, and they have to remember as many details about the sequence of events leading to a specific event (like purchase of a competitive product).

Get as many details from them as possible—who all were involved in the purchase decision, where they were when the thought first came to their mind, who they talked to about their decision, how they started the search and so on.

Ensure that you're not guiding their answers by asking leading questions. Your job during an interview is to listen impartially. Be careful of nudging people subtly towards answers that you desire. That's confirmation bias at play, and you'd be doing it without realizing.

It's true that one interview doesn't reveal much. But as you interview multiple people, you will start observing repeated patterns. (Perhaps you will realize that in your industry, people are much more driven by impulse than you imagined.) Such repeated patterns are the real nuggets of insights about people's true desires.

Yes, there's a risk in relying on memories too, as people can fabricate false memories without realizing that something they remembered never happened. However, the probability of a false memory is much less than the probability of a false reason.

> **Remember:** words are cheap and people use them liberally. Actions are where the truth lies, and the only way to get access to people's actions is to ask them to remember what they did, and not why they did.

STOP ASSUMING THAT YOUR CUSTOMERS WANT THINGS THAT YOU WANT

Mind projection fallacy happens when we assume that most other people are like us. It's an error to assume that they have similar desires and fears towards things as we do.

Normally, this is not such a big issue. The worst that can happen in most cases is perhaps an exchange of incredulous looks (for example, when a cricket fan encounters someone who doesn't know who Sachin Tendulkar is).

Don't model the world around your desires

But, for entrepreneurs, the mind projection fallacy is dangerous because it means they can end up working on the wrong problem.

As you can imagine, entrepreneurs are very different from non-entrepreneurs. They take more risk, have an unstoppable drive and they work hard to achieve what they want. They're also often early adopters of new products and services.

However, most people aren't like entrepreneurs. So, it's a mistake when an entrepreneur takes his drives as a norm for how all consumers behave. They assume that, like them, most people are driven, like to try new products and want growth.

Mind-projection fallacy happens because we have imperfect data about the world. When we fill in the gaps about someone else, we use our behaviour to predict how they would behave. That's fallacious because they might not have the same worldview or value system as you, the entrepreneur, has.

If you ever said, 'I never understand why people buy torn jeans', you've acknowledged the limitations of mind projection. People are very different from each other. Managers are not like executives. Teenagers in the US are not like teenagers in Canada. People who have done PhDs are not like those who have dropped out.

A practical tip on addressing mind-projection fallacy: assume you're not a model consumer. As an entrepreneur, you most likely are an outlier, not the norm.

Start by assuming you know nothing about target customers. Then start relying on hard, cold data to knit together your target customer's profile. Enrich the profile as much as you can. How do they decide? What's their budget? What are their goals? What excites them? What do they fear?

Understand their desires intimately, and acknowledge that your customers are likely nothing like you.

> **Remember**: overcoming the mind-projection fallacy is difficult, but it's the only way you'll form a less biased view about your customers.

THINK FROM FIRST PRINCIPLES BEFORE YOU INTERNET-SEARCH (OR ASK CHATGPT)

Like most technologies, search engines are both good and bad at the same time. They're good because they open up vast resources of information.

Today, our ability to know things instantly would seem like magic to previous generations. At the same time, precisely because searching is so easy, we've become habituated to googling for each little problem or doubt in our head.

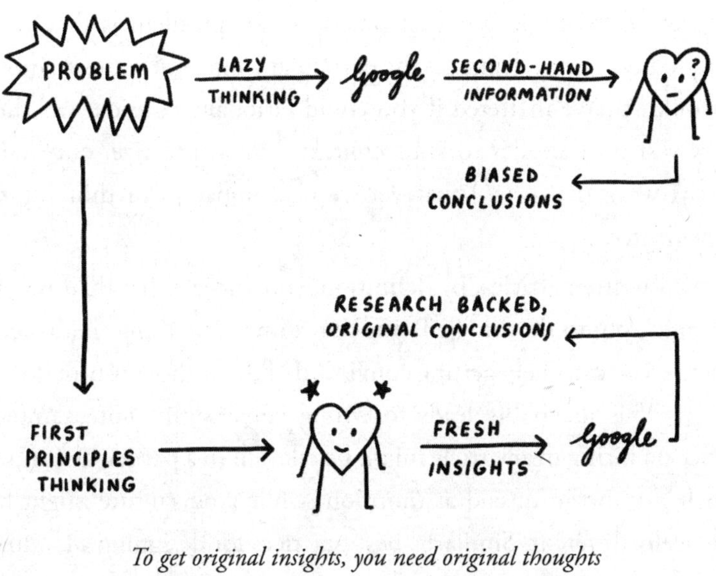

To get original insights, you need original thoughts

In programming circles, coding by internet-searching is popular, but this is equally true for all professions. Since search results are so fast and convenient, we are now slowly getting wired to automatically and subconsciously search-up any unresolved query in our head. This automatic reliance on search engines is dangerous because it is replacing our capacity for original thinking with second-hand information written by others.

It's important to note that articles written by others that show up on the search-results page are almost always biased. In fact, all forms of written material (including this book) are biased in some way because authors always end up overemphasizing their favoured perspectives. (In fact, typically, the opposite view isn't even mentioned.) So, when we search-up queries like 'how to design a landing page' or 'how to interview customers' or 'how to hire a marketing head', we get to read a particular point of view of an author.

Even if an article lists best practices, the problem is that such generic advice entirely misses the particular context of your situation. It wouldn't have mattered if you could rationally consider whether what you read applies to your context, but in practice, our brain doesn't work that way. Whatever we read impacts our thinking to some degree.

Well-written articles, by definition, convince us that their way is the right way to do things. If you're reading something that's well-written, you can't help getting convinced of the author's way of doing things. This inevitably leads to wrong conclusions. For example, advice on hiring in an article might be relevant in a particular culture which may be an unsaid assumption, while your culture might be drastically different. Similarly, best practices for designing a landing page might be contextual to SaaS or ecommerce, while you may be selling pharmaceuticals.

Why rely on second-hand info when you have a brain of your own? So, to prevent getting biased, *before* you search for anything on the internet, or ask ChatGPT, pick a pen and paper and write down your own analysis and conclusions about the problem at hand.

(And remember to always make a pros/cons list to systematically explore the opposite of your initial solution hunch.)

Only after you've put enough effort to think by yourself, should you internet-search. By doing original thinking first, even your research on the internet will be better, since: one, you'd have your particular context prepped up in the mind; and two, you'd be able to clearly think through whether the suggested solution will work in your context or not.

> **Remember:** the more effort you put in thinking upfront, the more nuanced approach you'll have towards solving the problem. Always approach problems from first principles and only then internet-search them to incorporate other people's views.

PART 14

BEYOND SUCCESS AND MONEY

WEALTH IS NOT MONEY, IT'S THE THINGS WE USE MONEY FOR

As an entrepreneur, money is obviously a massive motivation for why you're doing what you're doing. However, it's essential to understand that money is not wealth.

Wealth is the thing we want and by that logic, people can be wealthy even if they don't have a lot of money. In fact, because

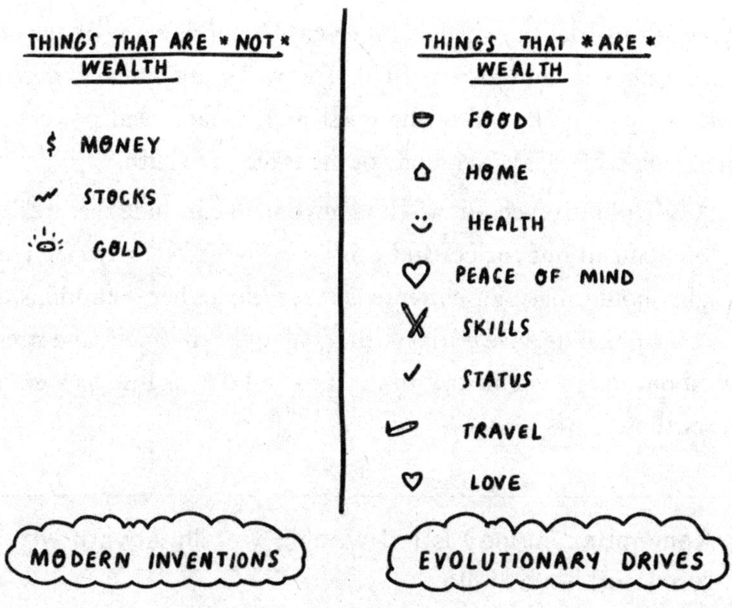

Money is not wealth

wealth is anything that is directly desired and attained, even animals and insects can be wealthy.

Money is popular because it allows us to acquire (certain types of) wealth. Money will be worthless if what you desire cannot be bought, or if there's nothing you desire.

Enough food, a decent house, good health and peace of mind doesn't require a lot of money. But a private jet certainly does. However, a private jet may not give as much satisfaction as something cheaper (like a good conversation with an old friend) may give.

In fact, if you're not careful, excessive money can work as negative wealth as it may drive away friends and family or as the anxiety of not losing all the money can cause continual mental turmoil.

Many entrepreneurs feel that the reason they're doing a startup is not because they want more money, but because they want to change the world. But changing the world is another way of playing status games in our society. In that way, it's not much different from money. As the old saying goes: money, fame and power are interchangeable. However, none of the three are wealth.

A careful introspection will lead anyone to conclude that wealth is abundant in our society and can be easily had by anyone. This insight should make an entrepreneur reevaluate her definitions of success and failure, give clarity to the goals of her business, and stress less about the inevitable day-to-day ups and downs that happen in all startups.

Remember: money is not wealth; wealth is what we want and have in life.

STARTUPS THRIVE UNDER UNCERTAINTY (OF THE RIGHT KIND)

Do you know how big companies make decisions? They build scenarios and models on spreadsheets.

They do this because often the decision-maker's job is at stake, so all substantial decisions by that person require justification, which is often derived from calculators.

But it's a myth that big companies don't take risks. Introducing new products is risky and so is expanding into new geographies. In fact, all decisions are risky in a way. (If they weren't, no decision is required, as it's simply obvious to all.)

Given that big companies take risks regularly, it's a miracle that startups exist at all. After all, big companies are better resourced, have established brands, and are better capitalized than startups.

So why do startups regularly keep popping up onto the scene and some of them even end up becoming big companies? That should be impossible, yet it's a regular occurrence.

Why?

The reason for this is that while big companies take risks, they hate uncertainty.

The difference between the two? Risk can be modeled and quantified on a spreadsheet, while uncertainty can't.

UNCERTAINTY IS WHEN SOMETHING IS BEYOND QUANTIFICATION.

It's what you feel when thinking about whether people will be ready to rent out their beds to strangers (Airbnb) or if anyone will ever buy a book without physically flipping its pages (Amazon).

Big companies cannot model the market size of people buying books online because it's completely uncertain (until a startup figures this out by actually doing it).

And because key assumptions cannot be modeled, big companies won't fund internal competitive projects until the uncertainty is fully resolved.

Often by that time, the startup has become too big to kill as it would have developed its own moats.

In this sense, uncertainty provides a cloud of fog that big companies systematically avoid.

What if the uncertainty that a startup is pursuing is resolved before business matures?

This often happens with inventors or discoverers who show the world that something hard is possible, and then someone better resourced ends up eating their lunch.

So, uncertainty about a key dimension of the business is good for a startup.

If everything is obvious and known about your startup, you need to ask why is no one else eating this obvious source of value? Is it possible that you're deluding yourself?

An important caveat about uncertainty is that since startups are poorly resourced, having too many uncertainties is also not a good thing.

Having one uncertainty is as good a deterrent as many, so a wise choice for an entrepreneur is to keep unknowns to a minimum (ideally just one).

These unknowns can range from technology viability to market acceptance to revenue models or go to market approach, which when resolved, works in favour of the startup.

The idea of uncertainty as the fuel for startup success has all sorts of unintuitive implications.

First, it explains why successful startups look like toys when they start. It's because successful startups have to feel unconventional. If they're too obvious early on, competition will eat them up.

Second, it explains why successful startups start by appealing to niche markets. This is because, for the mainstream market, solutions to obvious problems are already being pursued by big companies. For example, there's very little uncertainty in knowing that a higher mileage car will sell more and that's why big companies continue to push fuel efficiency forward. Tesla, a startup, survived because it wasn't certain how big a market there was for low-range, expensive cars that require a charger installation at home.

Third, it also explains why startups often commercialize existing technology and don't make fundamentally new inventions or discoveries themselves. That's because if a new technology, once invented, is known to obviously be useful (like better fuel efficiency), it's being pursued by big companies' R&D departments.

But if it's not certain if a new technology will be useful, then no investor is willing to fund the double whammy of market and technology uncertainty.

Sidenote: This is also why deep-tech startups have lower odds of success than conventional tech startups. It's because if a research area is well known to be important, deep-tech startups compete directly with thousands of researchers at better-resourced academic and industrial R&D labs.

To sum up, the following aspects seem to make up the recipe for a successful startup:

- Large uncertainty about a key business dimension
- Uses existing technology
- Pursues a niche market
- Unconventional, 'strange' offering
- Inferior current alternatives
- Builds strong moats while uncertainty is still unresolved

If there are multiple uncertainties, how should an entrepreneur resolve them?

Prioritize the most significant ones early on, when the (opportunity and funding) cost to failure is the lowest.

PS: This insight on uncertainty is due to Jerry Neumann, who writes an excellent blog.[1]

STARTUPS SHOULDN'T SOLVE TECHNICALLY HARD PROBLEMS

Startups get funded when they're expected to be valuable, and they're valuable when they can generate a continuous stream of profits for its investors.

With this view, the value of a startup comes mostly from its expected moat, that is, how well can it defend its business from competitors once they take notice of the market.

Startups that solve technically hard problems are often in an economically disadvantaged position because solving technical problems is hard, but once a solution is found, it's not as hard to understand or replicate it. And if the solution is the major value-driver of a startup but is easy to replicate by others, the value of the startup is diminished irrespective of how important a problem it is solving or how hard it was to solve that problem.

The usual tool for business defense for such startups is a patent. But patents (outside of pharma) aren't worth much. Patents are easy to work around and even if they're not, a startup cannot afford the multi-year, million-dollar patent litigation fighting others. No wonder, the majority of patents are deemed worthless by most studies.

One major exception to all that I've said so far is pharma or biotech. There, solving technically hard problems is a profitable strategy, and hence a booming VC and acquisition culture has evolved around such startups.

Why?

Solving hard problems in the medical domain is worth the effort because of three reasons: One, due to patents, competitors can't copy a molecule exactly so they have to modify it. Two, once the leading molecule is demonstrated to work via phase-one, phase-two, phase-three clinical trials, it has a lead time of five–ten years over competitors who will have to do their own trials because their substitute molecules differ from the original one and hence regulatory agencies require fresh clinical trials. Three, because the medical market is price-inelastic, margins are high and the original innovating startup is able to accumulate enough cash flow in the initial years to fight patent battles. So, the value of medical startups comes from the long regulatory period (and not necessarily from patents). Plus, it helps that people pay a lot for healthcare (as compared to other things they desire). Thus, medical or biotech startups can be seen as high-risk, high-return startups.

In contrast, most deep tech startups are high-risk, low-return startups. Low-return because, as we've seen, once a solution to a hard problem has been demonstrated, it's often easy to replicate (unless there's a regulatory agency with stringent criteria which implicitly gives an edge to the first one to solve the problem).

A beautiful case study of high-risk, low-return startups is the cleantech boom of 2000–10.

MIT has a report[1] where they analysed funded startups in this industry and found out that 90 per cent of them failed to return even their originally invested capital.

According to the report, cleantech startups had high risk in multiple areas: tinkering science takes time, so they were illiquid assets until then; expensive to scale, as building factories is capital-intensive; razor-thin margins, as they were competing against established commodity markets (oil and gas); and potential acquirers not ready to pay a premium as they figured they can develop technologies in house.

High-risk per se is not a problem (as demonstrated by returns in healthcare). But high-risk along with no or weak moat translates into low returns, which made cleantech a bad investment (in retrospect).

I worry that many upcoming 'deep-tech' companies (in synthetic bio, climate, food, among others) will face a similar fate to cleantech.

If you're building a deep-tech company, you need to answer what moat you're building and be honest with how strong it really is (patents are not moats).

Technical and scientific breakthroughs are essential to push our society forward but they often don't turn out to be great investments.

Hence, science/tech breakthroughs should be funded by the public (via govt agencies) and startups should comfort themselves in the roles of commercializing already available technologies (rather than inventing new ones).

To sum up, even though it's often the case that taking market-risk pays more than taking technical-risk, I don't think it's a useful classification.

Remember: think about the strength of your startup's moat once the scale of its innovations is widely known by many. If once the profit source is known, it isn't easily competed away, you have a valuable startup. If not, you have something cool (and potentially useful to society). But it likely won't become a successful business.

YOU CAN ONLY SUCCEED IF YOU KNOW HOW YOU CAN FAIL

We obviously want to always make successful decisions. Even though failure is often glamorized, nobody wants it on purpose. Everyone wishes to be successful whether they're starting a company, launching a product, or hiring a leader.

It may sound obvious, but the bedrock of good decisions is defining what good means before you pull the trigger on a decision.

Here's why it's important to define a clear, objective and unambiguous criteria before making any decision. First, without a commitment to an objective criterion, your brain will latch on to how you're feeling to decide whether the outcome of the project is good or bad. These emotions are influenced by all sorts of subconscious cognitive biases. In the end, you will be picking data points that support your emotional inclination while ignoring the other data points. This way, you'll miss all the important learning that comes along with the aftermath as big decisions.

An example of this is when you're hiring someone. Without clearly defining what success looks for a particular role, you may get increasingly biased by your likeness to a particular person. Since there's no objective criteria, you may start going with your hunch that's subconsciously biased by the way a person dresses, talks and other such criteria that we use daily to judge strangers. But a company isn't a tribal arena, and success in a job is most likely not a function of people's first impressions.

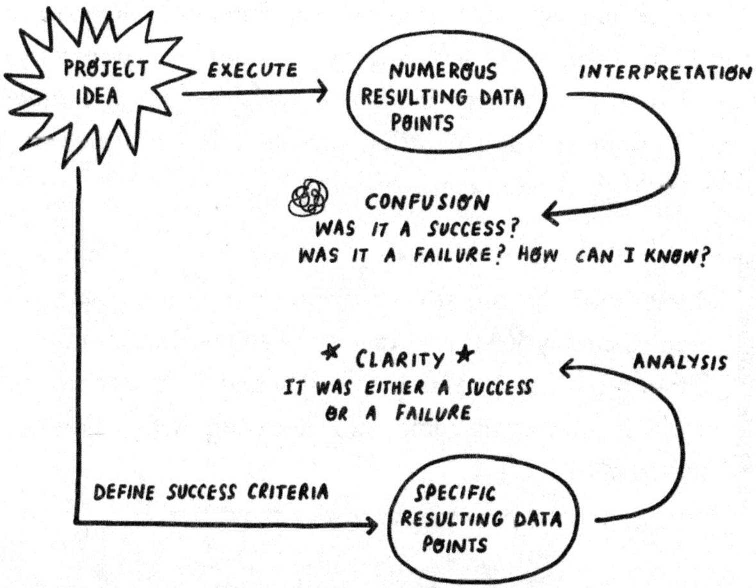

Success criteria has to be defined before a project starts, not after it ends

The second reason why an objective success criteria helps is that the task of defining what success means to you can shed light on the project plan, help you decide and even whether you need to do anything or not. Without defining success criteria, you're in the mode of 'let's do this and see what happens'. But what if you didn't need to do it in the first place? Suppose you force yourself to define a success criterion for a job before hiring someone. It's possible that your struggle with defining it tells you that it's impossible for a person to achieve what you're expecting her to do, or perhaps that such candidates don't exist in the market, or perhaps that your business doesn't need this role in the first place.

The third reason for an objective success criteria is that without it, there's no useful feedback or lessons for you to learn and improve. This is because without success criteria, there's no failure criteria, and without that, you'd never know where exactly you went wrong. You can only course correct in future if you have clarity and without objective criteria, you'd have lots of data points but no way to prioritize them for learning.

> **Remember**: before taking a major decision, always make sure you have a clear evaluation criteria. Otherwise, you're risking taking suboptimal decisions and at the same time not knowing why they're suboptimal.

YOU ARE A LOTTERY TICKET

Startups are like heat-seeking missiles, except they seek profit and live in a multidimensional world where one mistake means missing the target by a mile.

Startups are hard because they require several things to go right simultaneously. It's not sufficient to get one thing right, you must solve this multidimensional puzzle perfectly.

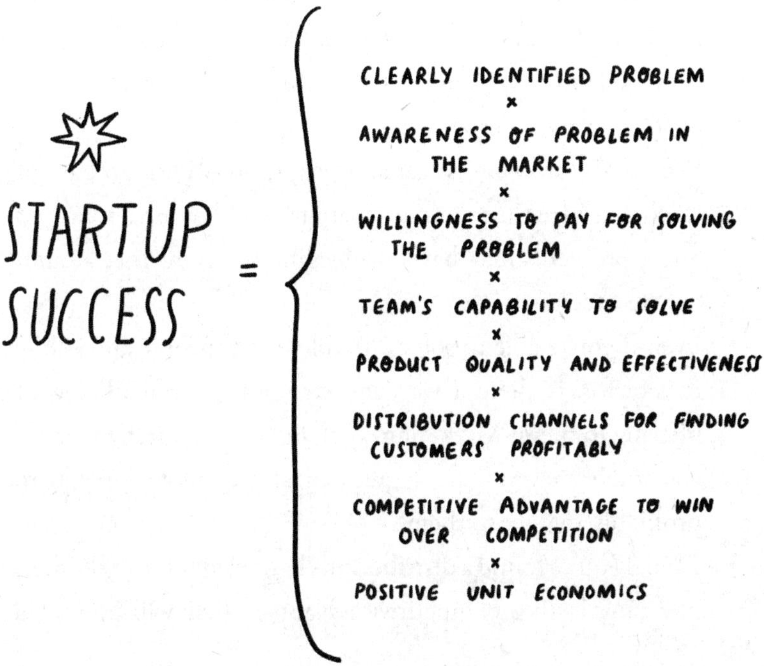

The startup stack of success

There are many things you need to get right, but these are the biggest ones that kill your startup if you don't get it right:

- Is the problem you're solving a real one, or is it just in your head?
- Even if the problem is real, are people actively looking to solve it? There are many problems that are merely inconveniences that not many people bother to solve. Is your problem one of those?
- Even if the problem has a high enough priority and people are looking to solve it, are they willing to pay for it? There are many problems which people want a solution for, but they'd not pay anything or much for it because they're habituated to expect a solution for free. For example, news and information is valuable to people, but people have come to expect to get it for free on the internet.
- Even if the problem is real and people are willing to pay for it, do you have the required capabilities to develop a solution? Some problems may have challenging solutions that are not easy to execute.
- Even if you're able to solve a problem that people are willing to pay for, is there a way you can profitably market your offering to them? Marketing costs money, and often potential customers may not be aggregated at one place for you to profitably market to them.
- Even if you've found a distribution channel, does your business have any lasting competitive advantage that will prevent a

bigger competitor or another startup from snatching your customers?

- Lastly, assuming you do everything right, will you deliver positive unit economics? Your business will struggle unless you're predictably generating cash flow.

Do you see how many things have to go right in order for you to succeed as an entrepreneur?

Our current society mythologizes successful entrepreneurs as gods. We have Hollywood movies getting made on this, their biographies are bestsellers, and media attention is constantly doled out on them. But do successful entrepreneurs deserve it more than unsuccessful ones?

Flipping the question, are unsuccessful entrepreneurs less capable than successful ones? Or perhaps they were simply unlucky?

The word 'luck' seems to have been banished from our modern society that assumes the world is perfectly meritocratic. But a moment of rejection will convince you that any outlier success has a huge random component that begins with where you were born, what chromosomes you have and what colour your skin has. Luck really does rule our world and to deny that is to simply set yourself against an unrealistic standard.

So, my dear entrepreneur, know that in your startup journey (and in life), there's only so much you can control. Success rates for startups are low, so don't get disheartened if this happens. You are as capable as any of the other celebrated founders out there. They got lucky, and may lady luck also smile on you!

Good luck.

> **Remember:** since so many things have to go right for a startup to be successful, it's foolish to beat yourself up if your startup doesn't succeed. With startups, failure is the norm and success is the exception that requires a healthy amount of luck.

NOTES

BUSINESSES EXIST TO FULFIL HUMAN DESIRES

1. Jeff Bezos, 2016 letter to Amazon.

PRODUCT-MARKET FIT REQUIRES DELTA 4 IN EFFICIENCY

1. SeedToScale, 'Kunal Shah's Delta 4 Theory of Successful Startups'.
2. Sean Ellis and Morgan Brown, *Hacking Growth: How Today's Fastest-Growing Companies Drive Breakout Success*, Currency, 2017.

WHAT ARE YOU BETTING ON: CULTURE OR TECH?

1. Joseph L. Bower and Clayton M. Christensen, 'Disruptive Technologies: Catching the Wave', *Harvard Business Review*, January–February 1995.

DEFINE YOUR MARKET AS NARROWLY AS POSSIBLE

1. Peter Thiel with Blake Masters, *Zero to One: Notes on Startups, or How to Build the Future*, Random House, 2014.

PEOPLE DON'T LIKE USING TECHNOLOGY

1. Free Press, UK, 2013.

EVERYTHING SOPHISTICATED ONCE WAS A PROTOTYPE

1. Mark Vaughn, 'Tesla's Little-Known Prehistory', *Autoweek*, 1 March 2021.

SWITCHING COSTS DETERMINE THE VALUATION OF YOUR BUSINESS

1. 'Berkshire Hathaway Shareholder Letter', 2007.

GENERATING PROFIT REQUIRES CREATIVITY

1. Leo Tolstoy, *Anna Karenina*, Penguin, 2003.

YOUR PRODUCT'S PRICE DETERMINES YOUR ENTIRE PLAYBOOK

1. Christoph Janz, 'Five Ways to Build $100 Million Business', *The Angel VC*, 5 October 2014.

ALWAYS SEEK DISCONFIRMATORY EVIDENCE

1. R.N. Shepard, *Mind Sights: Original Visual Illusions, Ambiguities, and Other Anomalies*, W.H. Freeman/Henry Holt, 1990.

STARTUPS THRIVE UNDER UNCERTAINTY (OF THE RIGHT KIND)

1. Jerry Neumann, 'The Illusion of Acceleration', *Reaction Wheel*, 7 October 2024.

STARTUPS SHOULDN'T SOLVE TECHNICALLY HARD PROBLEMS

1. Benjamin Gaddy, Varun Sivaram and Francis O'Sullivan, 'Venture Capital and Cleantech: The Wrong Model for Clean Energy Innovation', an MIT Energy Initiative Working Paper, July 2016.

ABOUT THE AUTHOR

Paras Chopra is an entrepreneur who founded Wingify, bootstrapped it from 0 to $50 million in revenue and sold it to private equity for $200 million.

Follow him on X: x.com/paraschopra

Read his blog: invertedpassion.com

HarperCollins *Publishers* India

At HarperCollins India, we believe in telling the best stories and finding the widest readership for our books in every format possible. We started publishing in 1992; a great deal has changed since then, but what has remained constant is the passion with which our authors write their books, the love with which readers receive them, and the sheer joy and excitement that we as publishers feel in being a part of the publishing process.

Over the years, we've had the pleasure of publishing some of the finest writing from the subcontinent and around the world, including several award-winning titles and some of the biggest bestsellers in India's publishing history. But nothing has meant more to us than the fact that millions of people have read the books we published, and that somewhere, a book of ours might have made a difference.

As we look to the future, we go back to that one word—a word which has been a driving force for us all these years.

Read.